CATFISH AND THE DELTA

CONFEDERATE FISH FARMING
IN THE MISSISSIPPI DELTA

Richard Schweid

Ten Speed Press
Berkeley, California

For my mother, Adele Mills Schweid, *and in memory of my father,*
Bernie Schweid, *and for their friend and mine,* John Egerton, *a man
for whom kindness is a reflex.*

1☺

TEN SPEED PRESS
P.O. Box 7123
Berkeley, California 94707

First printing, 1992

Cover design by Nancy Austin
Text design and typography by Wilsted & Taylor, Oakland, CA
Illustrations by Ellen Sasaki

Library of Congress Cataloging-in-Publication Data

Schweid, Richard, 1946–
    Catfish and the Delta : confederate fish farming in the
Mississippi Delta / Richard Schweid.
        p.   cm.
    ISBN 0-89815-454-5
    1. Catfishes—Mississippi—Delta (Region)—History.   2. Fish-
culture—Mississippi—Delta (Region)—History.   3. Delta (Miss. :
Region)—Social life and customs.   I. Title.
SH167.C35S39   1992
639.3'752—dc20   91-37671
                                                                      CIP

Printed in the United States of America

1   2   3   4   5   -   96   95   94   93   92

Acknowledgments

THIS BOOK's attitudes and mistakes are entirely the author's, but without the help and assistance given me by director Anice Powell and her staff at the offices of the Sunflower County Library in Indianola, and editor Jim Abbott and his staff at Indianola's weekly newspaper, *The Enterprise-Tocsin*, there would be a lot fewer facts in it.

There are people in this world who flat-out refuse to speak to a stranger, but, thankfully, they are awfully scarce in the Delta. Most people were open and cooperative, and willingly suffered, for free, through hours of my questions.

In addition, my thanks go to the following people who were kind enough to render various sorts of assistance along the way: Andree Akers; Andre Anderson-Walker; John Anderson; Saul Belz; Chris Carlson; Jonas Feld; Phyllis Frus; Mike Golden; Bill Harkins; Cathrine Hoemb; Dawn Miller; Emanuele Nastasi; Tracey Schubert; John Seigenthaler; Jim Sherraden; Kathy Starr; Dan Stein; Frank Sutherland; and Ornella Zoia.

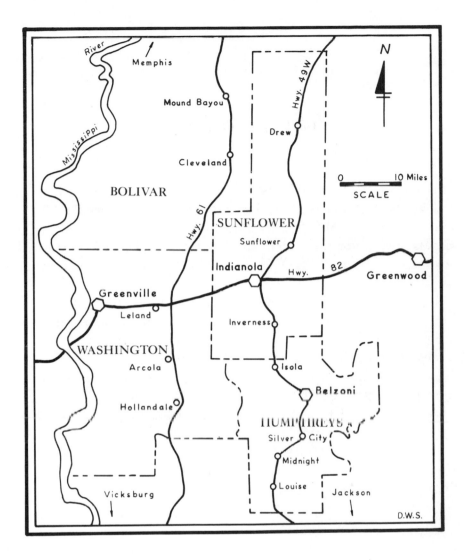

Table of Contents

CHAPTER I

Catfish Country

IT WAS early in the morning when I left Clarksdale, Mississippi, headed south on Highway 49 toward the heart of the Delta. I had an eye out for my first sighting of catfish ponds, as well as for a place to get a cup of coffee. But the farther I drove, the clearer it became that it was going to be a while before I found either one. The road was nothing more than a two-lane asphalt ribbon, with drainage ditches on either side, running through vast, flat fields of cultivated soil.

Northern Mississippi is divided into two parts by the Bluff, a ridge of land that begins just across the state line in Memphis, Tennessee, and runs like a spine with a western curvature down to

Vicksburg. In Mississippi, when people speak of the Delta, they do not mean the true Mississippi River delta, where the mighty river meets the sea south of New Orleans, but rather the low-lying flood plain of the Yazoo and Mississippi rivers, which lies west of the Bluff. It is a level, nearly treeless expanse of land some eighty miles wide and two hundred miles long between Memphis and Vicksburg. When the first white people settled there in the mid-1800s, it was a vast hardwood swamp that flooded each spring. The swamp was cleared acre by acre, and the flooding was gradually controlled by levees along the rivers.

It was spring when I went to the Delta, and the fields were dry and planted. There were seemingly endless rows of dark brown dirt mounded up, carpeted with the delicate, bright green of new cotton plants barely poking through the earth's crust. There were occasional winter wheat fields coming ready to harvest: huge expanses of waist-high emerald-green plants stretching to a distant horizon, waves of wind rolling across them. Mostly, though, the land was planted in cotton. I drove past mile after mile of ploughed ground, the rows of cotton flashing by the side window of my Volkswagen van with military precision. There were no other cars on the road.

This is deep country, a rural vastness so far back from the rest of America that it feels like a foreign country. The Delta is not on the road to or from anywhere. It is one of those places that has gone its own way, with its own character, its own culture. The only animal life I saw was red-winged blackbirds. They banked up out of the drainage ditches and away from the road as my van passed. Flushed suddenly up out of the ditches they'd come flying, vivid flashes of scarlet on the shoulders of their wings. The few signs of human life that I saw were unsettling: an occasional tar paper-and-wood shack at the edge of a field, with the ploughed ground coming right up to its walls. I would have thought these places were tool sheds had it not been for the unmistakable signs of human habitation — laundry strung up on a line between two aluminum poles at the edge of a field, or a dog on a sagging front porch scratching at its fleas. These

scenes reflected a poverty more severe than that of the inner cities; the tin-roofed shacks called up a bare-bones, rural living and a doing without things that most of us consider indispensable: health, privacy, education.

I passed a gravel turn-out on the right side of the highway where there was a ramshackle little wooden cabin with the word GROCERY painted on the gable. I pulled over, got out of the van, mounted three worn wooden steps to a tilted porch, and went through a screen door into the cool darkness inside. Along one wall was an old soda pop cooler, with chipped white paint and "Barq's" written in red script on its side, advertising a locally popular root beer. Next to the other wall was a low woodburning stove, and in the shadowy depths of the tiny room there was a counter. I felt eyes on me from behind it before I made out the small woman sitting there in the sprung easy chair with its ancient floral print upholstery. She was frail, with polished dark brown skin stretched tight over her birdlike bones, her fine grey hair in a plait on top of her head.

She answered my request in a deep Delta accent, slow, thick, and broad, shared by black and white, those intimate and flowing rhythms of unhurried speech as enveloping as the sweet smell of honeysuckle, speech with a resonance that wraps itself around you like smoke. "Used to have coffee in here many years ago, when I sold sandwiches and such, but there's nary a sandwich or coffee now.

"There's pop," she added, nodding toward the cooler, but I thanked her and left, holding out for coffee.

Farther down the road, I passed a sign telling me I had entered Tutwiler, and I took the first road to the right off the highway. It led me to a dead end in the middle of a town square surrounded by low brick buildings — all there was to downtown Tutwiler. There was a clothing store, a post office, and a hardware store, each still closed at seven in the morning. As I sat in the van and looked at the locked-up, empty town, the front door of a building across the street opened. A sign above the building's window read WONG'S SUPERMARKET. Out of the door came a tall, young black man in a white shirt

and black pants. He held the door for a wizened, tiny Chinese woman, who was following behind him. I approached them on the sidewalk and addressed myself to the woman, bending down slightly to do so, "Excuse me, is there anywhere around to get a cup of coffee?"

"We're not open and don't sell coffee here, not here."

"I know, but is there anywhere in town where I can buy a cup of coffee?" I asked, an edge of caffeine-deprived annoyance in my voice.

"No coffee here, we're not open yet," she said, insistently, as if I were hard of hearing or spoke some other language.

The man took pity on me. He had a vicious stutter. "Th-th-there's a Jit-jit-jit-ney Jungle down the highway. Th-th-they've got coffee."

A big, dark green Buick Electra 225 was parked at the curb, and he held the back door open for the woman. She was so small that she hardly had to duck her head to climb in the back seat. He got in front and drove away.

Sure enough, there was a Jitney Jungle convenience store less than a mile down Highway 49. I bought my coffee and watched a group of about a dozen black men of all ages, who were standing around outside waiting for someone to come by and hire labor for the day. A pickup truck pulled in, driven by a middle-aged white man wearing a green John Deere cap. He sat behind the wheel, the truck idling in neutral, while some of the men went up to his open window, presenting themselves for work. A handful of them climbed into the back of the truck, perching on the walls of its bed. The truck pulled off, leaving behind some of the men, who continued to stand, smoke, and wait to see if a day's wages would come their way.

I finished my coffee and got back on Highway 49. The road runs south, straight as a string. It wasn't long before my other morning's wish was fulfilled. Catfish ponds began to appear in fields beside the road: rectangular ponds, three times the size of football fields, spar-

kling in the sun. Each was surrounded by a graded levee wide enough to drive on in a pickup truck. A sign told me I was crossing the line into Sunflower County. Right on time, I thought to myself, looking at the catfish ponds. This was what I had come to see. They gleamed in the sunshine, big watery fields within fields. I was on my way to Indianola, the seat of Sunflower County, to learn about catfish farming.

Since childhood, I have been fascinated with farm ponds; the sight of them touches me in a way perhaps possible only for a city dweller, someone who loves to sit on the bank beside water and fish, but who lives in too urban an environment to have a readily accessible place to do it. That there were people who actually had their own ponds was powerfully impressive to me, even as a child. Swimming pools did nothing for me, but the idea of having your own wild piece of water was remarkable. For the pond-owners, I realized, it was no big deal — a place to let cows drink and to go fishing for a little bit when there was nothing else to do, but to have such a pond on the land where one lived seemed to me like riches.

The first farm pond I ever swam in belonged to an aunt and uncle in the North Carolina country. It was full of leeches. The first time I saw it, on a childhood visit, my cousins urged me in for a swim, then stood around giggling behind their hands as I stood for a long time barefoot on the bank, toes squishing in the mud, water dripping slowly off my bathing suit as my aunt picked the black, shiny leeches off my chest, back, legs, arms, and thighs and dropped them in a pail to be left in the sunshine, and scolded her children. Each leech she picked off left a blossom of blood behind as it was pulled loose from my skin. Even with such an unpleasant initiation, I spent many an hour of subsequent visits to my relatives fishing in that pond or just sitting beside it, watching its life: the birds, snakes, frogs, turtles, and dragonflies.

I was in Sunflower County to see what a whole land of farm ponds was like, to see what kind of world could encompass hundreds of farmers harvesting the water, making their living from the water.

The notion of a part of the country where substantial numbers of people spent their days farming fish fascinated me. It evoked a respectable labor that combined two of humanity's oldest occupations: fisher and farmer.

This was not my first trip to look at an aquacultural industry. I had been to southern Louisiana to see how people farmed crayfish ("crawfish" to the Cajuns) in flooded rice fields, and Martha's Vineyard, Massachusetts, to meet scientists who were growing lobsters in pens. Compared to catfish, crayfish and lobsters are small potatoes as aquaculture products. They are minor league efforts that have yet to make enough profits to guarantee long-term viability. It is tough to grow fish, crustaceans, and shellfish. There is uncertainty and risk at each stage. Things like disease, water quality, and marketing present a constant array of problems, and fish farming is much more difficult than just tossing a bunch of small fish in the water and keeping them fed until they are big enough to take out and sell. Many farmers who have tried growing something in water have lost their money, or teetered right along the edge of doing so.

Catfish farming used to be just as uncertain. The first commercial operations were in Arkansas, but they soon caught on across the river in Mississippi. During the first years that people raised catfish in the Delta, in the mid-1960s, a farmer might have had one or two ponds he fed by walking along the levee, carrying a pail full of feed and broadcasting it out on the water by hand. By 1990, catfish had become a sophisticated, megabucks aquabusiness. There are almost 100,000 acres of catfish ponds in the Delta—where more catfish are grown than in all the rest of the world—and they generate more than $300 million in annual revenues. This was something I wanted to see with my own eyes.

After all, to satisfy the appetites of the world's meat-eaters by giving them farm-raised catfish instead of beef, pork, or poultry makes good sense. While a cow eats almost eight pounds of feed to produce a pound of meat, a pig four pounds, and a chicken three, it only takes two pounds of feed to grow a pound of catfish. In addition, the feed

is made from grain and is usually unmedicated, which means that people can eat catfish without consuming the potentially harmful, incidental doses of antibiotics that are routinely fed to cattle, pigs, and chickens.

Because the pellets of catfish feed float, and the pond-raised fish are trained from birth to do their eating at the pond's surface, they do not go searching for food down near the bottom, which is how wild catfish spend most of their lives. The low-cholesterol meat of the farm-raised fish is firm, white, and neutral in taste, completely lacking the strong, fishy, bottom-feeder flavor of a river catfish. The water that goes into the ponds is from artesian wells and has repeatedly tested squeaky-clean.

In the United States, the drive has always been to make the ground tillable, to farm the land and not the water, so this country lags far behind in aquacultural experience. Fish farming is an ancient profession, and records show that the Chinese were raising carp as early as 1100 B.C. While carp are generally thought to have been the first fish farmed, aquaculture of a sort was being practiced in Europe during the Middle Ages. Records from the world of Charlemagne around 800 A.D. indicate that fish were netted in rivers and kept alive in ponds until their presence on the menu was required. There were trout farms documented in Germany in the 1700s. Trout were also "the fish of the czars," and they were raised by Russia's royal family. In the late 1800s, the Cambodians were growing an Asian species of catfish.

In our own time, aquatic husbandry seems to many people an attractive way to make money. A variety of factors make it look like a good investment: people are eating more fish and seafood because they believe it to be healthier than red meat; overfishing and pollution are reducing the nation's supply of fish caught in the wild; and many uses to which land has profitably been put in the past are no longer money-makers. Between 1980 and 1990, people across the United States spent large amounts of time and energy and money trying to become commercial producers of such diverse species as

redfish, catfish, striped bass, crayfish, lobsters, mussels, tilapia, trout, salmon, shrimp, oysters, prawns, and clams.

Of them all, the only unequivocal success was the channel catfish *(Ictalurus punctatus)*, the no-count, no-class slob of the whole bunch, unkosher because it lacks scales, uncouth because it is the goat of the fish world and will devour anything: a slippery, slimy-skinned croaker. These charms notwithstanding, the nation's consumption of pond-raised, grain-fed catfish grew from virtually none in 1965 to about 400 million pounds a year in 1990, far and away the most successful aquaculture in the United States.

The Delta's catfish industry is vertically integrated: Many of the feed plants and processing plants are owned wholly and cooperatively by the farmers who grow the fish in ponds. A number of ancillary businesses have grown up around the catfish industry, from hatcheries to net makers to pond builders. A ten-acre catfish pond is about four feet deep and can easily hold sixty thousand fish, which will take eighteen months to grow to the marketable size of 1.5 pounds, with the price being usually between seventy-five and eighty cents a pound. Catfish farming is not something that people do on a small scale. Less than eighty acres of ponds is considered to be a waste of time, and most farmers farm three to seven hundred acres of ponds. If all goes well—and there is plenty that can go wrong — a farmer's net profit is $500 to $700 per acre, a profit of at least $150,000 a year.

The success of catfish farming has most profoundly affected two Delta counties: Sunflower and Humphreys, where more catfish are grown than anywhere else in the world. Running more than one hundred miles between them, the southern border of Sunflower is the northern border of Humphreys. This is incredibly fertile land, where cotton was king for more than a century and where share-cropping and tenant farming were ways of life longer than anywhere else in North America. In the late 1980s, the revenue produced by catfish surpassed that generated by cotton, and, for the first time in the twentieth century, cotton was not the most profitable of Delta

crops. The number of acres under water grew year by year, and the number of acres planted in cotton diminished. At the same time, the catfish industry supplanted cotton as the largest employer in Delta towns like Indianola.

Many people in the Delta found close parallels between farming cotton and farming catfish, not the least of which was that they both create a local economy made up exclusively of the well-to-do and the poor, where the rule is excessive wealth or bare survival. Critics of the Mississippi catfish industry contend that it continues a long tradition of keeping a large group of black Deltans dependent on minimum-wage labor for their income, keeping them poor and, frequently, uneducated in order to have a ready labor pool. In 1990, poor people still lived in Sunflower and Humphreys counties in conditions of abject poverty worse than what was found in some Third World countries. The infant mortality rate for Sunflower County was higher than that in Chile, Cuba, or Malaysia. Humphreys County had nearly three times more infant deaths than the national average.

Memphis, sixty miles north of Clarksdale, is really the beginning of the Mississippi Delta. It is not only at the tip-top, but serves in many ways as the Delta's capital city. Memphis is full of people who came from the Delta and who still have family, land, or business there. The Delta has fed and nourished Memphis with people, produce, and culture, and has kept the city's bankers, brokers, and builders busy. Cotton was traditionally marketed in Memphis, and many of the cotton industry's largest fortunes were made in the Delta. In addition, Memphis was the first way-station for the Delta's best and brightest black citizens who decided to leave home and seek their fortunes elsewhere. For those who left because they could no longer stand living under Jim Crow, and there were many of them, Memphis (the Bluff City, as it is called) was the first metropolitan

area they reached. Today, it has a large and successful black community that is firmly rooted in Delta soil.

And Memphis has long been the Delta's party town. It has always been the first place where white Delta planters have come to enjoy their riches and exhibit their legendary propensity for spending money in search of pleasure. Like the planters, Memphis is also where black Deltans come when they can afford to go looking for a good time. There is a long history of "getting down" in Memphis, and for black people during the first half of this century that meant going to Beale Street, a quarter of nightclubs and crowded sidewalks where anything could happen. People in the Delta do not need any special occasion to come to Memphis, either. Dinner and a movie are considered more than enough of an excuse to make the hour-and-a-half drive from Indianola.

The music that Memphis has contributed to the world—through the blues clubs and juke joints that used to thrive on Beale Street—is built directly on a foundation of Delta blues. Blues music, like so much else from the Delta, made its first stop in Memphis, coming up with the partygoers. Performers like Elvis Presley, B. B. King, and Jerry Lee Lewis all learned their music there. It is fair to say that the roots of rock and roll are in the Delta, birthplace of the blues.

The best way to leave Memphis for the Delta is not Interstate 55, which runs down to Jackson beside the Bluff, at the eastern edge of the flood plain. No, the best way is to aim straight for the heart and go down the same route that the blues came up when they came north. Start on Third Street in downtown Memphis and head south out of town. Soon, the street narrows down to two lanes and becomes Highway 61. Follow it an hour south to Clarksdale, where Highway 49 branches off and the deep Delta begins. The landscape flattens out and opens up, the vistas get broader, and there is nothing to see but cultivated land from horizon to horizon.

It is not like that east of the Bluff. There it is hill country: wooded hills divided into small family farms, generally peopled by frugal, God-fearing Baptist Mississippians. The land is fertile, but suffers

from severe soil erosion. The people who work it have a tradition of providing for themselves, taking care of their own, and asking help from no one. They butcher their own livestock, hunt squirrels and coons with a vengeance, grow their own vegetables, and heat their modest houses with wood, which they have carefully thinned out from their own small stands of timber. They are, by and large, a sober lot, and those who drink regularly in public do so at the risk of their social standing in this world and their soul's repose in the next. Hill folks are parsimonious in almost all things, an exception being the amount of money they might be willing to pay for something as eminently sensible as a fine blue-tick coon hound to use for hunting raccoons through the deep brush and woods at night.

West of the Bluff is the Delta: a low-lying flood plain, flat and fertile. The difference in terrain between the Delta and hill country is matched by the difference in the people who live in them. Deltans tend to take life in considerably larger doses than their compatriots to the east. They farm bigger tracts of land, live faster, drink harder, and spend more money. Much more money. A family from the hills is not likely to be pleased if a favorite daughter announces plans to marry a man from the Delta.

This is a strain of Mississippi prejudice that does not revolve around race; both black and white Mississippians hold the same stereotypes about people from the hills and those from the Delta. Both black and white folks will admit that there are some nice people from the other region, but they will also tell you that they would not like their sons or daughters marrying one of them. In fact, a hill family would probably prefer a Yankee for a son-in-law to someone from the Delta. At least Yankees are known for their thrifty ways. Conversely, Delta families would be more likely to welcome a Cajun from Louisiana than someone from the hills, because they know that Cajuns are relaxed and like to let the good times roll.

"You know, people from the hills just don't want much to do with people from the Delta," said one black man from Coffeeville, a hill town eighty miles northeast of Sunflower County, whose job had

brought him to the Delta. "People who live in the Delta are held to be shiftless, no-count, immoral, lazy, gamblers, and drinkers. Every time I go home, people look me over real carefully to see if I've picked up a bunch of bad habits."

The Delta was the last wilderness to be claimed in Mississippi, and most of it was still an uncharted cypress swamp a century after the hill country was settled. The people who finally came to drain and clear it were largely from the hills, dissatisfied with the lack of opportunity in a region already divided up and which had severe soil erosion resulting from intensive cotton farming. It was usually desperation that drove folks to try and make a place for themselves in the malarial Delta, but there were some things that could be said for it. It was a true land of opportunity, different from the hills in the sense that there were no dales, draws, and hollows where each family struggled to make its small parcel of land produce enough to live on. When the Delta was settled, there was as much land available as a person had the stomach and resources to work—first with slaves, later with mules and sharecroppers, and still later with tenants and tractors.

I, myself, was ambivalent about moving to the Delta, even though I only planned to stay a few months. The idea both attracted and repelled me. I was lured by the rural quality of life there and the treeless, open beauty of it. I looked forward to spending some time in a place where the rhythm of life still came from the demands of agriculture. And there was no question that the Delta was producing the most successful fish farms in the country. This was the place where people had finally learned to make money by growing fish. Indianola seemed like the logical headquarters from which to gain an understanding of how catfish farming worked and how it affected the people who worked at it. The town—supposedly named by early white settlers for an Indian princess named Ola—was within a thirty-mile radius of the ponds producing 85 percent of the nation's farm-raised catfish. The world's largest catfish processing plants were in or near Indianola, as were the two largest producers of cat-

fish feed, which together milled more than $80 million of feed pellets a year. If you wondered what catfish farming was like, this place was the heart of the matter.

On the other hand, I knew that to go to the Delta was to confront the complex and often agonizing relationships between black and white Americans in the deep South. I grew up in Nashville during the early 1960s, when the civil rights movement was in full swing, and I was taught early by my parents that black people were no more nor less human than white people, no better, no worse, and not much different. All the people of other races whom I have known since then—those I loved and those I did not—have only strengthened that conviction. Every American should have known this simple truth by 1990, but I was well aware that this belief would not be shared by most of the white people I met in the Delta, particularly not in Indianola, a prominent town on the map of the Aryan nation, one of the cradles of the doctrine of white supremacy. The White Citizens Council was born there in 1954, in response to the federal Supreme Court's order to desegregate the schools.

My knowledge of Mississippi was scant. When I was growing up, I thought of it as a benighted state, racist and retrograde. Any time I drove to New Orleans from Tennessee, for instance, I would schedule the Mississippi stretch of the drive for the daylight hours. Don't let the sun set on you in Mississippi if you're in a car with out-of-state plates, is what I used to think. It was the place where segregation remained a moral issue for white people, as much a matter of principle as of economics. Despite, or perhaps because, of this history of hate, there is also a tradition of people coming from outside Mississippi to investigate life in Indianola. I was not the first person to decide it was a good representative specimen of a small Delta town.

In 1935, an anthropologist from Yale named Hortense Powdermaker came and lived in Indianola, studying the lives of the town's black women and, through them, the culture of the Delta. She lived nine months among the women, doing interviews, attending

church, sharing their lives, and learning about their joys and sorrows. In the book she wrote, *After Freedom*, Powdermaker gave the town a false name: Cottonville. Her prose is academic, accurate, and clear, painting a portrait of the black women in Indianola at that time that shows them to be strong and resourceful in living their lives and raising their families under adverse, oppressive conditions. For most of these women, this Jewish anthropologist from Yale was the first white woman who had ever found any strength, purpose, or value in their lives.

Two years after Powdermaker left town, a sociologist named John Dollard, who was a colleague of hers at Yale, came to Indianola for five months and wound up with a book called *Caste and Class in a Southern Town*. As a social document, it is considerably more limited and less human than Powdermaker's book, probably because Dollard did not have access to the black population as Powdermaker did. Dollard could not, as a white man, go to visit black women in their homes nor could he interview them in public. Black men generally wanted little to do with a Yankee prying into their lives, and he only overcame their mistrust to a limited degree.

In 1964, a Connecticut illustrator named Tracy Sugarman wrote a book called *Stranger at the Gates* about his time spent in Sunflower County during "freedom summer" as an illustrator for *Life* magazine. This white, middle-aged man accompanied northern college students, black and white, who had come to register Sunflower County voters at the courthouse in Indianola, and he vividly describes the life he found in the Delta. The same time is documented in a forthcoming book by *Los Angeles Times* staffer Kay Mills about the life of civil rights heroine Fannie Lou Hamer. Born in Ruleville, in northern Sunflower County, Hamer left a lifetime of working for a cotton planter and led the voter registration movement in Sunflower County. She was a driving force in the Mississippi Freedom Democratic Party, which integrated the state's Democratic party.

These books document life and death in Indianola, and issues far more serious than catfish farming. But if their authors could spend

time in Indianola, so could I. Something about the Delta drew me strongly. From the first day I crossed into Sunflower County I was energized by its deep isolation from urban life, drawn to its huge sky, and amazed at how little the land had changed since 1964, when Sugarman described it, or even 1935, when Powdermaker lived there.

One of the things that *had* changed since those books were written was the presence in the landscape of catfish ponds. They sparkled in the sun, some the brown of river water, others a shining aquamarine, more the color of the Mediterranean than of the Mississippi. Despite the occasional group of ponds, the vast majority of the land is still dry, still planted in soybeans or cotton.

As I drove, a yellow biplane flew low across the road in front of me, swooped down just above a field covered with the new green of young cotton plants, and released a puff of herbicide from its tail, which settled down on the plants as the plane banked steeply up and away. I was to see the same thing many times again. Crop dusters in yellow biplanes laying down their toxic mists are a common sight all over the Delta. A portion of each chemical with which the fields are bombarded eventually washes out of the soil and into the Mississippi, contributing greatly to bottled water sales downriver as far as New Orleans, where even the poorest people put aside enough to buy drinking water for their families. Thanks to a natural clay cap on the local aquifer, however, the chemicals do not get into the water that feeds the catfish ponds. There are only minute traces of herbicides and pesticides in the water of the catfish ponds, and none in the meat itself, according to state regulatory officials.

The first settlement of note that I came to in northern Sunflower County was not a town, but rather Parchman Prison Farm, the Mississippi state penitentiary, rendered infamous through the years by its work songs and blues, a prison with a reputation every bit as bad

as any other in the nation, equal in despair to places like Angola in neighboring Louisiana and the nightmare maximum-security federal prison in Marion, Illinois, that replaced the island of Alcatraz as this nation's warehouse for its most intractable cases. PARCHMAN PRISON FARM, read a green highway sign, DO NOT STOP NEXT 2 MILES. It was enough to give me a shiver, like swimming through a cold spot of water.

Parchman did not have the foreboding stone walls topped with concertina wire that surround most penitentiaries. There were no ramparts with searchlights and gun turrets. Instead, 4,800 state inmates were housed on eighteen thousand acres of empty Delta farmland, wet in the winter, sweltering hot in the summer. The prisoners lived in complexes of small low buildings.

A substantial part of Sunflower County was cleared by convict labor from Parchman, and many of its roads were built and maintained by chain gangs. In addition to the hard labor under the merciless Delta sun and the water moccasins and rattlesnakes that occasionally lay in wait for the unwary laborer clearing the canebrake and timber, Parchman had a particularly nasty system of discipline. It appointed certain inmates to the position of trusty and had them oversee the others in the fields. The trusties were allowed to carry pistols, but they more frequently enforced discipline with a broad leather strap called a Black Annie. Their cruelty is said to have far exceeded that of the guards hired from outside, whose own reputation was pretty bad. The practice of using trusties as guards did not come to an end until 1974, following revelations about an incident in 1970, when an inmate died working in a cotton field. His death was listed on the books as due to sunstroke, but a legislative committee determined that he had been shot by a trusty. This official finding led to the abolishment of the trusty-guards and their replacement by 383 newly hired civilian guards.

Work at the prison farm today is just that: farming. What mostly is grown at Parchman, aside from the vegetables and meat to feed the prisoners, are row crops of cotton and soybeans. Plenty of the land

at Parchman would hold water well and would make excellent cat-fish ponds, but there are no fish farmed there and not likely to be any in the future, regardless of the potential profits to the state. For one thing, the profits are only potential, while the capital outlay required to get into catfish farming is always substantial. Fifteen ten-acre ponds cost over $300,000 to get started, and at least a year must pass before any fish reach a marketable size. The other reason catfish farming would not work at Parchman is that it is a twenty-four-hour-a-day job for seven months of the year. Prisoners at Parchman work during the day and get locked up at night, a schedule definitely unsuited to the rhythms of growing catfish.

CHAPTER II

Ponds of the Delta

INDIANOLA, POPULATION 11,500, is located at the junction of two of the Delta's most important roads: two-lane Highway 49, running north to south, and Highway 82, a four-lane artery between Green-wood, on the eastern border of the Delta, and Greenville, fifty miles to the west on the Mississippi River. Highways in the Delta do not actually pass through towns, so much as run beside them, with the town's homes and and older downtown businesses tucked off to one side of the road. Indianola's stretch of Highway 82 is lined with convenience stores, fast-food franchises, and motels to attract the cross-Delta traveler. It also has a large corporate supermarket, two discount stores from nationwide chains, and a liquor store to bring Indianolans out to the highway.

The first thing I noticed, driving around the quiet, tree-shaded streets of the actual town, was that I had never been greeted so frequently in a place where I was a complete stranger. It did not matter if I was among the broad avenues and stately homes of the white residential neighborhoods, in the downtown business district, or on the narrower streets with the somewhat shabbier houses on the black side of town. People everywhere acknowledged my presence with a friendly salute. Whether they were in cars passing in the opposite direction, were walking down the street, or were standing in their yards, people who met my eyes raised their hands in greeting. It continued to amaze me for the three months I lived in Indianola—everyone waved, black and white, when you met their eyes.

Deltans have a well-deserved reputation for liking to socialize, for being gregarious people. Maybe it is because they are so far-flung across such a large, open space. They may live far apart, but distance is no barrier to their social lives. People think nothing of driving forty miles to have dinner with a friend. The idea of not going to a party or a softball game because it will take half an hour to drive there is deemed absurd.

Indianola itself is a relatively small town, and people frequently run into their friends and acquaintances during the course of a day's business. A few minutes here and there spent chatting with friends are not considered a waste of time, but rather the punctuation marks in a workday. Nowhere is this more evident than at the post office. There are no mail carriers for downtown Indianola's stores—every business and professional person has a box at the post office. There is residential delivery, but most people do not give out their home addresses, preferring to get their mail at a box in town.

"I just don't like to get my mail at home," one attorney told me, as we stood talking in front of the bank of postal boxes in the lobby of the Indianola post office, surrounded by pairs of other people exchanging the latest news of their families and businesses. "It doesn't feel right. I like to come here for it."

This attitude is held by a lot of Indianola's citizens, black and

white, and it means that just about everybody runs into just about everybody else on one or another day at the post office. There is rarely a moment, from its opening to its closing, when at least two Indianolans cannot be found in conversation at the post office, either inside by the boxes or outside on its broad steps. The post office is conveniently located at the north end of the row of stores that make up Indianola's main downtown street: clothing stores, a Piggly-Wiggly supermarket, a pawn shop, a bank, and a drug store.

The post office means a lot to Indianolans, and always has. In 1892, President Benjamin Harrison, a Republican, appointed Minnie Cox as postmaster when he could not find a qualified white Republican for the job. Cox was a black woman from a respected and prominent Indianola family, who, with her husband, founded the first black-owned savings bank in Indianola. She held the position of postmaster through three Republican administrations, praised by each of them for the efficient way she performed her duties, but in late 1902, the whites of the town banded together and called for her resignation. The mayor and sheriff of Indianola told her they could not guarantee her safety, and she resigned. In retaliation, President Theodore Roosevelt closed the post office for nearly a year, after which he gave in and appointed a white man to the job.

From the Indianola post office, I could be in deep country in any direction within a five-minute drive. Even in town there are numerous houses, in both black and white neighborhoods, that display the ways of the country, with corn, pole beans, and tomatoes coming up in large backyard gardens and old, shady pecan trees growing close around the front porches. When I drove for just a few minutes, the town with all its trappings dropped away, and there was nothing to see but earth and sky and cotton fields on either side of the road. It was like being able to cross a border into a foreign country in a mat-

ter of moments. No place in Indianola is very far removed from the great stretches of land that surround it.

If it were not for the occasional patch of cypress swamp in a particularly low-lying spot, or a short bridge passing over a bit of bayou, it would be impossible to imagine that all this cultivated land once stood in swamp, canebrake, and hardwoods, and that it remained mostly that way until the end of the nineteenth century. The job of clearing it was done chiefly by black men using crosscut, two-man saws to cut down the trees, mules to drag them out, and fire to burn them. The low ridges, which had the best drainage, were the first to be cleared, their first-growth cypress trees felled and put to the torch to make room for a crop. Once fields were broken and growing cotton, the bottom land was cleared until, finally, every tree was uprooted and every square foot of available soil was drained and planted.

It was not easy to subjugate the Delta to a plough. The land was exceptionally inhospitable, and that is why settlers waited so long to attempt it. The hill country was being farmed well over a century before much ground was broken in the Delta. In addition to its nearly impenetrable landscape, numerous dangers awaited those brave, foolhardy, or desperate enough to try living there. Bears, panthers, and venomous snakes were abundant, and they were accompanied by the most lethal denizen of the Delta: the anopheles mosquito. Malaria was pandemic. Many people died of malarial fever, particularly those who were very old and very young, and in the most vulnerable states of health. Many more walked around with it, incapacitated by harsh chills and fevers when it ran through the most virulent part of its sixty-hour course, and were left feeling miserable and debilitated, even after it had passed. It was as easy as going outside to be bitten and reinfected. In 1915, malaria comprised about 60 percent of the cases of illness treated by physicians in the Delta.

Lots of the Delta's first white settlers were men who had left their families behind in the hills rather than expose them to the terrible

living conditions west of the Bluff. The first thing they did was build sawmills. Then they cleared hardwoods from the land and planed them into boards with which to build houses and barns. Even after they had their homes built, these early settlers often continued to live alone. The more people they saw die of "swamp fever," the more reluctant they became to bring their families.

The extraordinary fertility of Delta soil was a settler's reward for the hardship of clearing the land. Until the late 1800s, when serious efforts to construct a system of flood-control levees began, each spring brought a flooding of most of the rivers in the Delta, backed up by overflow from the Mississippi River. The flood waters of the Mississippi annually brought a few inches of America's finest topsoil, which had been washed into the river by melting snows and spring rains from land as far north as Minnesota and Illinois. Each year, the river spread out above its banks from Memphis to Vicksburg, depositing topsoil and leaving layer upon layer of the finest farmland in the country, free of charge. In some places in the Delta, the alluvial topsoil is over twenty-five feet deep.

For the first half of the twentieth century, Delta land grew the best cotton in the country, and while more cotton was produced in California and Texas, nowhere was it a more important part of a state's economy than in Mississippi. With large holdings of land and sharecroppers to work it for almost nothing, Delta farmers made money. After the Second World War they began to diversify, adding soybeans and rice to their list of crops, but cotton was still king. Gradually, as equipment began to get more costly and the expense and size of the chemical component grew, farms got larger and larger, fewer and fewer.

Despite the fertility of their soil, Delta farmers were vulnerable. They had been growing row crops on an agribusiness scale, and went deeply into debt in order to buy more land and more equipment during the prosperous years of the 1970s, before interest rates rose and exports fell. Cotton farming was built on a credit system, with the banks making their loans at the beginning of the season,

and the planter doing likewise, providing a "furnish" to any tenants or sharecroppers on the farm. Then, when the crop was brought in, the worker paid the planter, who paid the bank. During lean years, a farmer's debt load increased, but for the planter who could hang on long enough, there would be some fat years to offset them. Farmers were encouraged to think there would be no end to the cycle of growth. Lending institutions like banks and farm credit associations encouraged farmers to borrow money and increase the size of their operations.

"Son, they were giving away money back then," one Indianola farmer told me. "They'd come right out to the fields, you didn't even need to go into town. They'd draw up the papers and write you a check right there in the truck. They made it hard to turn down."

However, the boom was short-lived. It was not long before inflation brought interest rates up, which combined with the rising rate of the dollar in the international marketplace to bring an abrupt end to the good times. Cotton and soybean profits depended heavily on foreign sales, which began to dry up. American textile mills, unable to compete in the world market, closed down in record numbers, further reducing the demand for Mississippi cotton, while $8-a-bushel soybeans began their long slide down to end at $4 in 1990.

What ensued in the state of Mississippi was not a slight decline in farm profits, but an unqualified disaster. In 1979, the value of row-crop revenues in the state was $737 million. Four years later, in 1983, it was $181 million. It did not take long for the banks and credit associations to get nervous about the size and number of the loans they had out in the agricultural sector. They began calling in their paper and putting a freeze on new money available to farmers.

Up to that point, there was nothing unique about the plight of Delta farmers. It was the same one faced by farmers all across the nation who had bought the get-bigger-or-get-out theory of farming during the 1970s and were being forced out, as a result, in the 1980s. But unlike the millions of farmers elsewhere who went under during those lean years, many Delta farmers were saved from ruin. Saved

by the land itself—by its ability to hold water—and by the lowly catfish. An inhabitant of Mississippi since prehistoric times and long taken for granted as an occasional part of the diet, first by Native American dwellers in the Delta, then by settlers of African and European descent, the catfish was certainly nothing special, but it was catfish that saved many a Delta farmer from foreclosure.

There are two principal kinds of soil covering the Delta. The first, and traditionally the most favored by farmers, is sandy loam—a fine soil that drains well and is found closest to creeks and rivers because it is the first to silt out when the water overflows its banks. This is the kind of ground that cotton loves to grow in, and sandy loam in the Delta can produce as much long staple cotton per acre as just about anywhere else in the world. The second class of soil is called buckshot. It is farther back from stream banks, has a higher clay content, and drains poorly. Buckshot is usually not planted in cotton, but perhaps in soybeans or some lesser crop, or simply left fallow. There are too many days and weeks of rainy weather when buckshot becomes unworkably wet and muddy. But while this kind of ground may not be any good for growing cotton, it is great for farming catfish, because its high clay content and impermeability make it just right for holding water in ponds. This meant that farmers who wanted to try their hand at growing catfish did not need to use good cotton land for their ponds. They frequently had some buckshot acreage just sitting idle.

It is not cheap to start a catfish farm, however, even for those who do not need to buy extra land to get started. A 1988 bulletin from the state estimated that eight ponds covering fifteen acres apiece (considered by most to be the minimum number of ponds worth fooling with) would cost well over $200,000 to dig, fill with water, and stock with two-inch fingerlings. The fingerlings can be bought

from a catfish hatchery, of which there are a number in Sunflower and Humphreys counties, for about a penny per inch. To feed those eight ponds until the fish in them reach the marketable size of one and a half pounds, which takes about a year, will cost another $150,000. So before the ponds are ready to be seined for the first time and their contents sold to a processing plant, about $400,000 must be invested in them.

These high start-up costs did not prove to be as much of an impediment in the Delta as they would have been in other parts of the country. The area's farmers and their bankers were used to doing business in six figures. A cotton combine costs $100,000 at the local John Deere dealership, and just about everyone who plants any kind of crop has one. Likewise, an eight-row cultivator. And annual operating expenses, including chemicals, fuel, and seed, are high. An annual trip to an institutional lender was one that Delta farmers were accustomed to making, just like their parents, and their parents' parents before them. They accepted a lot of debt as part of life, and were able to enjoy a good night's sleep despite owing amounts of money that would keep most folks awake staring wide-eyed into the darkness. Farmers in lots of places would have balked at taking on more debt when they were already on the verge of bankruptcy, but Delta farmers did not hesitate. When it began to look like there might be some money to be made growing catfish, they headed first for the bank and then began digging ponds.

"I remember when I first put in a few ponds back in 1980," a Sunflower County catfish farmer told me. "My banker was keeping a close eye on me. He was kind of nervous about it. I put a few big grass carp in each pond. He'd come out to look everything over and I'd walk along the levees with him and throw a little feed on the pond. Those carp would come up and I'd say to him, 'Bunch of big ones in there.' He'd go back to the bank feeling good."

It was quite an accomplishment to make a banker feel confident about having loans out on catfish ponds. In fact, that kind of loan

portfolio was the sort of thing that makes a banker's stomach clench with anxiety. The long wait between making the initial investment and having a single fish to sell in the marketplace is nervous-making. During the growing period, there is no way for a banker, or anyone else, to know how many fish are in each pond or how they are faring. The wait for a return is also trying because it is not hard for a bad farmer—or just an unlucky one—to lose a lot of fish, and lose them fast. It is perfectly possible for every fish in a pond—say $50,000 worth—to die in an hour. If the oxygen level in a pond should drop and the farmer does not notice it and promptly oxygenate the water, the fish will suffocate. There are also a number of other, slower ways to lose a pond of fish, including diseases, predators, and excessive algae.

Nevertheless, Delta bankers, like their customers, were used to risking large amounts of money on agriculture, which was always something of a crap-shoot itself, even if the crops were growing in fields where you could watch them. Thus it was that during much of the 1980s, local banks were more or less willing to advance loans to catfish farmers who wanted to expand their operations, and even to row-croppers who wanted to turn some buckshot into ponds. The person who wanted to expand could often get a loan using the fish in existing ponds as collateral. (By the end of the 1980s, however, a combination of bad experiences and increased scrutiny of their loan portfolios by federal regulators put an end to this easy money, and bankers would no longer accept fish as collateral.)

Catfish farming in the Delta is clearly not a small-scale, sustainable aquaculture. It is done on a scale every bit as grand as cotton, and the stakes being won and lost are just as high. It takes both money and nerve to get into catfish farming, but a lot of Delta farmers who had spent their lives being cotton planters were able to make the adjustment, and they will testify that it saved them from foreclosure.

Take Larry Cochran, for instance. In his late forties, he is big,

with a rugged, squared-off jaw and an easy laugh, and he has spent his adult life working the same piece of the Delta that his father and grandfather worked before him, outside the town of Isola in northern Humphreys County. In 1980, he grew a thousand acres of cotton and soybeans. By 1985, he had stopped row cropping altogether and was growing over two million pounds of catfish a year in thirty-three ponds. By 1990, he had forty ponds, twenty-three of which he farmed himself, and seventeen that he leased out.

"I started messing around with fish back in 1978," he told me. "Me and my brother put in four ponds. Then the row crops like to broke me. I was still paying off my debts, years later. Fish are the only thing that saved me from going belly-up."

While fish have been successful for Larry Cochran, they certainly do not give him a debt-free life. The expenses associated with farming twenty-three catfish ponds are enormous. The fish begin eating heavily when it warms up in May and grow increasingly voracious as the temperature rises, then slowly taper back as the year moves toward the fall. From November through April they may eat only once a week or so. At the height of the summer's feeding season, however, Cochran spends $30,000 every two weeks for feed, and puts twenty tons a day in his ponds. "It's amazing when you think of the numbers involved," he said. "I remember my grandfather borrowing eighty thousand dollars at the bank for a year to buy his seed and get a few hundred acres of cotton planted. He could feed both his and my dad's families, and now it costs me sixty thousand dollars a *month* to feed twenty-three ponds of fish."

What was important to Cochran, though, was that fish make it possible for him to keep going. For a while, it looked like the family would have to get out of farming and he would have nothing but debt to pass on to his son, Kevin. Then he began farming fish, and when Kevin graduated from college there was a place waiting for him. When I met the Cochrans, Kevin was managing part of the operation and had begun a family of his own. It looked as if the family

would be farming in Isola for a while yet, and that knowledge was deeply satisfying to both father and son, regardless of their debt load.

Humphreys County runs from Isola, just below its northern border, to Louise, just above its southern, and covers 421 square miles. More catfish were grown there in 1990 than anywhere else in the world, some ninety million pounds of them. Billboards marking the northern and southern county lines feature an illustration of a market-size channel catfish—its gun-metal blue, grey, and silver colors looking clean and appetizing—and big letters informing travelers that they are entering the CATFISH CAPITAL OF THE WORLD.

If one had to designate a capitol building for the catfish capital, there's no doubt about where it would be. The movers and shakers in the world of catfish farming can be found at the Pig Stand, a little barbecue joint at the side of Highway 49 on the outskirts of Belzoni (pronounced Bel-zona by most locals), the seat of Humphreys County. The Pig Stand is where policy for the catfish industry gets shaped and deliberations go on every day but Sunday. Beginning early in the morning and continuing throughout the day, the pickups come and go in the gravel parking lot around the place. Farmers come in and pour coffee for themselves out of the pot on the counter into one of the chipped, heavy, white porcelain cups from the stack beside it and order a biscuit and sausage from the short, black woman who works behind the counter. Outside, by the side of the road, is a big sign between two tall poles. It lights up at night to show a ruby-red heart within a triangle with bright white lettering below reading: BELZONI, THE HEART OF THE DELTA.

Inside the Pig Stand a lot of space is taken up by the big, brick barbecue oven that is built into the wall behind the counter. There are a few long tables, around which the collective worth of farmers sitting on soda-fountain stools in cotton work clothes and short-

billed caps is generally in the tens of millions. They meet each other at the Pig Stand in the mornings as they drift in and out for breakfast or a second cup of coffee after breakfast eaten at home; then around 10 A.M. they stop by for a quick coffee or Coke on the way to town to get a part or see someone; then again after the midday meal for another coffee; and once more when they need to come back into town around 3 P.M. for something else and stop in for one of those exceptionally tasty barbecue sandwiches to appease an afternoon appetite. All the while, news and gossip is exchanged; word travels remarkably fast from the Pig Stand. There is nothing of any importance that happens to catfish farmers in Humphreys County—and as Humphreys County goes, so goes every catfish farmer in the Delta—that is not general knowledge pretty soon after it first gets mentioned.

The Pig Stand is at one end of what author Tony Dunbar described as Belzoni's "segregated pig," in his book *Delta Time*. Blacks are not made to feel welcome there, and while a one-time passerby on Highway 49, who happened to be black and hungry and stopping in for some barbecue, would be served, black Belzonans do not eat there. Local citizens of color patronize Wimp's, a barbecue house across the tracks. The barbecue from Wimp's is a shade better to my taste, but the biscuits from the Pig Stand are the lightest and best I have ever eaten.

Powdermaker wrote in 1935:

> The chief difference between the outlying landowners and the townsfolk [of Indianola] is that a few of the former employ managers to relieve them of regular and continuous work. Leisure as the prerogative of the white gentleman is an old southern tradition; but the white planter of the community who enjoys comparative leisure has not taken over the aristocratic conception of what to do with one's time. For the most part he spends it drinking Coca Cola at the drug store, or just hanging about town. *After Freedom*

Most white Delta farmers are still pretty much the same way, as I saw when I was there. They don't do much of the actual hands-on

labor of farming, whether they grow row crops or catfish. Which is not to say they don't work hard and have plenty of stress, but the calluses on their hands are more likely to have come from being wrapped around the steering wheel of a pickup truck than a tractor. They do drive out to the fields or ponds frequently during the day to see how work is progressing and make plans with a foreman for what the next day's work will be, but mostly what they do is manage. This kind of farming can be done by a woman with as much success as by a man, but there are few women in the Delta who choose farming for a career. Many women, however, have found themselves with a farm on their hands when their husbands died, and many a Mississippi widow has done perfectly well managing a farm in her late spouse's stead. To date, only a couple of women have inherited and continued to work catfish farms, but as the first generation of male catfish farmers dies off, it is quite likely that the numbers of female fish farmers will increase.

Like the cotton planters before them, farmers still make the decisions, give the orders, sign for loans at the bank, and take the profit or loss. Theirs is the worry and the risk, but their daily work is not in the fields. Not that growing cotton or catfish is an easy way to make a living. There is plenty to worry about. But a goodly portion of a farmer's day is spent in town making deals with other farmers, picking up the mail at the post office, talking, telling stories, and staying on top of paperwork, which can be a full-time job, alone, in these times. Ever since the price per pound on the world cotton market sank below what an American farmer could grow it for, the only way to make money growing cotton has been by negotiating the tortuous, ever-changing route of crop subsidies from the federal bureaucracy. That kind of paperwork can keep a body busy farming morning to night without ever getting near the fields.

Federal money has not played much of a role in the growth of the catfish industry, although the town of Sunflower successfully applied for a $400,000 federal urban development grant when the Grain Fed processing plant, a farmer's cooperative, was built in

1984. The actual physical labor of catfish farming is simple and can be performed by hired help. The ponds need to be maintained, and the grass needs to be cut around the levees in order to keep the snake population down. The fish need to be fed, and there are a host of small maintenance jobs on equipment like generators, aerators, tractors, nets, and the array of other things needed for the job.

I heard white farmer after white farmer lambast the federal welfare program for the poor and rant against the way in which single, black, teenage mothers "cheat" and "abuse" the system of welfare checks and food stamps. "I was behind a colored girl in the checkout line the other day, and she paid for a box of salt with a one-dollar food stamp, then got outside and threw the box away 'cause she just wanted the change," one cotton planter told me in an indignant, how-the-poor-rob-our-taxes voice.

But these same cotton farmers and their families also had money to spend thanks to the nation's taxpayers. In 1990, each family cotton corporation could receive a federal subsidy of up to $50,000, depending on how many acres of cotton it grew. Families form different corporations using different configurations of family members and land, and each of those corporations is eligible for a $49,999 subsidy payment. Delta farmers call this a Mississippi Christmas tree. Without those subsidies, there would hardly be a boll of cotton grown in Mississippi, yet the farmers bitterly resent a poor Delta woman who has children out of wedlock to increase the size of her welfare check.

The toughest work in catfish farming comes during the months between May and November, when the oxygen levels in each pond must be monitored three or four times a night. Once the sun is down, the algae in the pond stop photosynthesizing—they consume oxygen but do not release it. If the day has been warm, the oxygen consumption is accelerated, and on those nights the level of oxygen in the pond may fall below two parts per million. Unless the pond is aerated promptly, all the fish in it will suffocate. It is critical that each pond be monitored and its oxygen measured every two or three

hours, but the work is monotonous and lonely. Oxygen checkers need to sleep during the day, and this is not a farmer's idea of fun. What bestows on a catfish farmer the kind of planter status and life-style that Deltans esteem is the ability to hire enough crew and trust-worthy supervisors to check and aerate the ponds so that the farmer can sleep the night through.

If a Sunflower or Humphreys County farmer works with his hands, he is probably black. The approximately one hundred black farmers in the two counties tend to have smaller tracts of land than their white counterparts and to work them with their families, hiring as little extra labor as possible. The number of black farmers in the Delta is higher than in most other places, but there is cause for alarm when it is compared with two decades ago. The black farmer is disappearing here at the same precipitous rate as in other parts of the country. Going, going, virtually gone.

The loss of farming as a possible occupation for African-Americans is a national reality, just as it is for Euro-Americans. Farming is something that only corporations, or wealthy individuals can afford to do. Most black Americans are excluded from the land's stewardship, the same land that many of them worked so long and so hard. Twenty years ago there were probably a hundred black farmers in Humphreys County, and now that number is around fifty, according to county agent Eddie Harris. It is a trend that shows no sign of reversing itself. "The black farmer is in a real decline, moving toward zero," Harris told me. "The main reason is that they don't have the collateral the bank wants for loans and they are forced to get out of business."

The catfish industry was not much use to those black farmers who did manage to hang on to their land during the early 1980s. They could learn to grow catfish as well as white farmers, but lending institutions were unwilling to loan them the capital to dig and stock ponds. I found only one black catfish farmer in Sunflower County and only one in Humphreys. This, despite the fact that black people consume an estimated 75 percent of the catfish sold each year. This

figure is coming down slowly, as more white people try farm-raised catfish for the first time, but a national telephone survey funded by Mississippi State University in 1989 found that 60 percent of black Americans have eaten catfish for a meal, compared to 43 percent of whites. Given that blacks make up only about 13 percent of the population, the health of the catfish industry is disproportionately dependent on the continued business and goodwill of African-Americans.

Still, that is life in the Delta, where the survival of a white minority in the style to which its members are accustomed has always depended in great measure on the presence and cooperation of a large number of poor black citizens. The catfish industry reflects this, but it is by no means atypical. Until the 1980s, white people in towns like Indianola controlled most of the elected offices and the municipal pursestrings, as well as the land and the factories. People of both races continue to live parallel lives, Delta lives, side by side, but separately.

Downtown Indianola, with its courthouse, its post office, and its few blocks of low brick stores and offices, looks a lot like many another small southern town. What sets it apart from the others is the Indian Bayou (Deltans pronounce it "by-oh," unlike their Cajun neighbors in Louisiana who say "by-you"), a real cypress swamp that winds smack-dab through the center of town.

By the 1960s, decades of neglect had turned this bayou into more of a town dump than a town treasure. For years, Indianolans had been protesting its gradual degradation, and they finally decided to act. Fifty thousand dollars was appropriated by the town's board of aldermen to clean, clear, and widen it. The banks were leveled, which allowed them to be mowed to discourage snakes; clumps of cypress trees were left undisturbed in the middle; and a weir was built at one end so that the water level could be regulated.

Once the people of Indianola had cleaned it up, they found Indian Bayou a joy to behold from numerous vantage points in town. Lots of houses in Indianola have the bayou running through their back yards, and there are three different bridges that cross it downtown, so there are numerous places along one's daily route that afford a look at a stretch of bayou. There is something evocative and pleasing about cypress trees standing in water—their knobbly knees sticking up through the surface around them.

Indian Bayou has resident flocks of mallards, wood ducks, and Canadian geese, along with great quantities of turtles, who sun themselves on logs sticking out of the water, and snakes ranging from many nonpoisonous species to the occasional water moccasin (although they generally prefer the peace and quiet around the catfish ponds). One day, in the part of Indian Bayou that flows across the street from the courthouse, I saw a nutria swimming with its mouth full of green leaves. On another day, an eleven-year-old boy fishing with worms across the street from the Boy Scout headquarters caught a six-pound largemouth bass. And on still another day, a ten-foot alligator crawled out of a small bayou named Mound Bayou, and took up a position stretched out on Highway 49, just eight miles down the road at the town of Inverness.

The bayous also grow mean mosquitos, and Deltans have suffered from their bite, even, one presumes, in prehistoric times. Mosquitos, however, were probably nothing more than a minor annoyance to the Native Americans until malaria was introduced by the European explorers. In 1541, Hernando De Soto's expedition encountered the descendants of the mound builder tribes that had been in the Delta since 1500 B.C. The Spaniards brought them malaria, syphilis, and smallpox, which spread rapidly. By the 1700s, when the French arrived, the tribes were decimated by swamp fever. The French adopted the Indian name for the river—Yazoo—which meant "River of Death."

Science has since eradicated malaria in the region and returned Deltans to their pre-Columbian state of suffering mosquitos only as

a minor—and nonfatal—torture. For the uninitiated and unaccustomed, the Delta's mosquitos have a bite that leaves a welt the size of a golf ball, which itches like crazy. Every year, as the weather gets warmer, mosquitos come out in increasing numbers. It becomes almost unbearable to be outside at dusk without wearing "dope," which is what folks there call mosquito repellant, as in: "Honey, did you use dope on the kids?"

Nevertheless, Delta children are always getting out without it, running around wearing shorts and a T-shirt at most, and their legs—rich kids' and poor kids' legs alike—are continually covered with mosquito bites. Middle-class adults, black and white, refuse to give their blood as a meal in order to be outdoors, and will not submit willingly, meaning that they will not spend an evening grilling steaks in the backyard unless they are doped up and safely under a lethal pale-blue bug light emitting the nearly constant sound of sizzling insects.

Some people told me that the mosquitos were getting worse and blamed the increasing number of fields flooded to grow rice, while others said the catfish ponds were to blame, and still others said the problem was not getting worse, but had always been just as bad. No one disputes that mosquitos were plenty bad right along. And why not? There has almost always been plenty of standing water in the Delta, regardless of the season, and standing water is what mosquitos like best. A person can grow to love living in a practically treeless landscape and even adjust to excessive summer heat, but there is no peaceful coexistence with mosquitos, and they are cited by one and all as the worst drawback to life in the Delta.

As one might expect in a region plagued by mosquitos, people there are exceptionally fond of the purple martin, that fork-tailed member of the swift family, which can eat its weight in mosquitos every day. A store-bought martin house resembles a miniature metal apartment building on a pole, with six or nine holes to a house, and many people have them in their yards. Even more numerous than the store-bought models are the homemade martin houses fashioned

from large, home-grown gourds. A hole is cut toward the bottom of the gourd's fat end and a wire wrapped around the gourd's narrow neck, which is hung from another wire strung between anything convenient: a tree and a pole, or a corner of the house. Although one of these gourds is a single-family martin dwelling, they are usually strung close together so the birds can live in tandem. There is a low vacancy rate for martin homes, and straw, denoting a nest inside, sticks out from each hole. Put up a martin house and it will be filled quickly; hang a gourd and it will soon be occupied. A farmer described to me what happened when he first saw his future wife: "I went to her like a martin to a gourd."

Spring moved rapidly toward summer during my stay in the Delta, and the days grew steadily hotter. I love to walk, but in the Delta, walking in the heat of the day is not something one does by choice. Five minutes in the bright glare of the sun is enough to beat you down, drag you out, and leave you panting and exhausted. The only time it is possible to enjoy a walk is early evening, as the light falls and the mosquitos are not yet out in force. Then the air is cooling, a soft breeze comes up, and it is worth doping up to go outside. Sunsets in the Delta are slow and frequently spectacular, the sky above the flat land going through a number of pastel shades before flaring to gold over the dark fields. There is usually an hour or two, those hesperian hours just before dark, when it is wonderful to be out walking.

I rented a house for my stay in Indianola, a large antebellum home with a big front yard on Western Avenue, so close to downtown that the post office was only a five-minute walk, yet I could walk the other way and in ten minutes be in the country. I did this many an evening, on a route that took me out of town, past the white kids' baseball diamonds, and into open ground where the road runs straight, as far as the eye can see, between two immense fields: one planted

in cotton; the other lying fallow, overgrown with tall, yellow, black-eyed susans and mottled with patches of the dried-blood color of dock weed. Indianolans take their Little Leagues seriously, and as I passed by the ball parks the cheers and shouts were loud, gradually fading as I walked out the road.

The ditches were much more noticeable on these walks than when I drove past them in my van. On foot, they appear as an important part of the landscape. They are broad and deep, on both sides of the road, dug there to drain the water from the fields. The dredging of these ditches, along with the felling of first-growth timber, was a primary labor of clearing the swamp and making it arable. They are called "grudge" ditches—black English for "dredge" ditches—which is what they were originally called by those who made them. During my walks, a string of splashes would precede my steps along the road, as frogs on the banks of these grudge ditches, hearing me coming, jumped one by one into the water.

Every so often a vehicle would pass, frequently a pickup with a black Labrador retriever riding in the back, a .22 across the rifle rack, and a a young good old boy behind the wheel. Just as frequently it would be an older-model American sedan—a long, low Buick or Oldsmobile—with four middle-aged black men in it, each wearing a baseball cap, and a bunch of long cane fishing poles extending from a rear window. If the vehicle passed me going the other way, the driver, black or white, would always raise a hand to greet me as our eyes met.

Redwing blackbirds perched overhead on the telephone wires, cheeping and peeping their limited but strident repertoire as I passed below. Martins swooped and dived across the fields. The road I took crosses Indian Bayou south of town. This part of the bayou is not cleaned up or cleared, and a toxic-looking green scum covers its surface, empty beer cans bobbing here and there. Plastic bags of garbage have been tossed down on the overgrown bank, and I once saw that someone had abandoned a broken-down sofa with stuffing leaking out next to a cardboard Heineken box with the hind-quarters of a dead dog protruding from the box flaps. Dumped by

some son of a bitch who was too lazy even to bury his own dead dog. (It is hard to imagine that a woman might have left it there, practically impossible to imagine a woman who would do that.) Farther on, there was a stretch of grudge ditch where I often flushed a mallard duck. He would take off down the ditch, heading toward the bayou, staying low, flying fast, wings beating hard.

CHAPTER III

A Million Dollar Tongue

EACH APRIL, there is a World Catfish Festival in Belzoni, the seat of Humphreys County, a town of slightly more than three thousand people. The festival is promoted heavily throughout the Delta, and a lot of people make the ninety-mile drive north from Jackson, or west from Oxford. About forty thousand attended in 1990. Downtown Belzoni is about two blocks square, and the first sign of festivity I saw when I got there, around noon on a Saturday, was a lot of people walking in the streets and a thin man wearing dark glasses sitting on a metal kitchen chair out on the sidewalk, an old, broad, fire-engine red Gibson electric guitar across a skinny thigh. He was set up in front of a big plate glass window with TURNER'S PAWN SHOP,

MONEY LOANED ON ANYTHING OF VALUE written across it. A sign on the store's door read: IF YOU'RE SKIPPING SCHOOL, SKIP THIS PLACE TOO—WE'LL REPORT YOU TO SCHOOL AUTHORITIES.

The man in the chair was a blues singer named John Paul, and a group of older men stood around him, passing a brown, pint-sized paper sack. John Paul did not look as old as most of the others, but a hard-lived life was written on his face in a scar beneath his eye and another in the middle of his forehead, which had a cross-hatch pattern as if a hot metal grid had met with his skin. His eyes looked permanently bloodshot. Somebody passed him the paper bag. He upended it quickly and gratefully, passed it along, and got back to playing.

(It does not have to be that way. James Son Thomas, sixty-seven, who was the Delta's premiere living bluesman in residence when I was there, told me, "I used to think I had to be drinking to play the blues, but in the last two years I've found out different. I can play without it. I never would have believed it, but I can play without drinking.")

John Paul had a small, crackly, portable amp beside his chair. He did not look like a man whose life had brought him great happiness, but he sure could play the blues. I listened to him get all over a Muddy Waters tune, "Forty Days and Forty Nights," with a long, wicked, bottleneck riff between verses, and it was obvious he knew his way around the blues side of his guitar's neck. It was toe-tapping, soulful music.

Two blocks away, there was a stage mounted in front of the steps of the Humphreys County Courthouse, which was draped in red, white, and blue bunting. There were long tables with plates of barbecue, beans, and coleslaw for sale. People were sitting in folding chairs on the courthouse lawn. There was a group of cloggers onstage: white, teenage girls, dressed in identical short red-and-white skirt outfits clog-dancing to "Rocky Top." Booths were set up in the middle of both of Belzoni's streets. This was the festival's flea market, and its booths offered every imaginable useless thing for sale.

One booth, for instance, was chock-a-block with machine carvings of an unpainted wooden bird on a branch, "Welcome to Our Nest" printed on the bottom. They were selling briskly. The streets were full of people browsing the booths.

I walked back to the pawn shop. There was still a small crowd of black people standing around John Paul's chair, listening to him play. Two well-dressed, middle-aged black women passed by and stopped to dance, caught by John Paul's bottleneck, a soulful slide up the strings in the middle of Jimmy Reed's, "You Got Me Running," which had the women into a shake and dance step almost before they knew it. They danced for a minute, laughing, then moved on down the sidewalk.

A white man and a young boy stood hand-in-hand by one of the booths and watched the two women move to the song. The man was perhaps forty, in a white, short-sleeve shirt and khaki slacks. The blond-headed boy beside him wasn't older than eight. "They're having a good time, aren't they?" the man asked the boy, as if they were at a zoo and he was speaking of a separate species.

The World Catfish Festival was one small, local component of a broad strategy to market catfish to the seafood-consuming sector of the American public, a job that required some doing. If there was ever a fish with a poor reputation among people with money in the big cities, it was the catfish. Even in the rural South, where people have always eaten it, pan fish like bass or bream are considered superior in taste. In many places outside the South, catfish were simply not found on the lists of food people had tried in their lives. Lots of people in the North and the West were born, lived, and died without ever tasting one bite of catfish, or wanting to. This was particularly true for European-Americans, although even African- and Asian-Americans, who did occasionally eat bottom feeders, often preferred drum or carp to catfish.

A catfish from the wild has a strong, heavy, fishy flavor. It is an omnivore, equally happy to eat plants, bugs, smaller fish, and just about anything else it can swallow. It spends most of its life browsing for these delicacies near the mud at the bottom of the water where it lives, and its eating habits are reflected in the taste of its meat. People who like the flavor of river catfish do not have much use for the pond-raised variety. One such person, who has eaten catfish all his life, summed it up scornfully: "You touch a farm-raised fish and your hands don't even smell. A fish should stink. River fish stink. They stink like fish 'cause they're down there eating other fish."

Fortunately for catfish farmers, this attitude is rare. For most Americans, the less a fish tastes like fish the more they like it, and farm-raised catfish fill the bill. They do not have a muddy flavor, nor a fishy flavor. In fact, their white, firm meat is just about as close to no flavor at all as a fish can get, and the farmers are proud of that.

On the farm, catfish begin eating grain in the hatchery troughs on their fourth day of life, while they are still fry and look as much like pollywogs as they do fish. Their feed looks like fine dust. After six days in the hatchery they are moved to an outdoor fingerling pond, and by that time they have already made the two critical adaptations necessary to grow up with a different feeding behavior and flavor than a channel catfish in the wild: food is at the surface, and there is always enough to go around.

Feed for adult fish comes in small round pellets about the size and color of dry dog food. The pellets are distributed by a blower, which is mounted beneath a hopper on the back of a pickup truck. A farm hand drives the truck slowly along the top of the levee, and the feed is blown from the hopper out over the water. The pellets float on top of the pond, thanks to the toasted corn in them, and the catfish come up for them. As the feed rains down, the placid water of the pond comes alive with the sleek, dark bodies of catfish rising to the surface. This is the only time of the day that the healthy inhabitants of a pond will reveal themselves—fish at the surface any other time sig-

nal disease—and farmers often like to drive along behind the feed trucks and get a glimpse of their fish at feeding time. The grain fills all the dietary requirements of the fish, and they have no desire to search for sustenance at the bottom of the ponds.

These grain-fed fish have a bland taste that is pleasing to the majority of American palates. Filets are the way most newcomers to catfish like to eat it: a fish with little flavor and no bones, perfectly adapted to the consumer's quest for "convenience." Catfish filets are something you can bring home from the supermarket at the end of the day and bake, or microwave, and have on the table in short order with no preparation time. But, in order to want to do this, the American public first had to be convinced to taste it.

The catfish industry recognized that introducing the fish's new taste to the public would not be easy, but it persisted and was able to make real progress in replacing a negative public image with a positive one, using the tools of modern advertising to get its message out. This marketing is done primarily through the Catfish Institute, a nonprofit entity headquartered in Belzoni, funded by a "check off" at the Delta's two feed mills of six cents for each ton sold. Beginning in 1987, the institute hired a Manhattan advertising agency, which mounted a campaign to put catfish on restaurant tables and in supermarket seafood departments nationwide. By 1989, a consumer survey showed that of all the people who had heard of farm-raised catfish, almost half of them knew it was "different" from wild catfish.

With more and more people willing to try catfish at least once, it is incumbent on the industry to rigidly maintain quality. A person from Boston or Boise, who has lived a lifetime without ever tasting catfish and then lays out four dollars to try a farm-raised fish, is only going to give it one chance. If that person gets a "bad" fish, there will not be a second opportunity, and if the first one is good but the second bad, there will not be a third purchase. If restaurants are not convinced that there will be a steady supply of consistently high-quality fish, they will not put catfish on their menu. Thus quality

control, in order to ensure a uniform product, is essential. Unfortunately, what and how a catfish eats are not the only things down on the farm that play a hand in determining how that fish will taste.

There are two large categories of "off-flavor," which is the industry's term for farm-raised fish that do not have the optimal neutral taste. The less frequently encountered type of off-flavor results from water that has been contaminated by diesel fuel. This often comes from tractors out by the levee. If the oxygen content falls drastically in a pond at night, it is aerated by large paddlewheels attached by a long shaft to a tractor drivetrain. The tractor is left idling on the levee to turn the paddlewheels out in the pond and may run all night. There are always tractors parked or standing on the levees, and some spillage of fuel into the water is inevitable.

Most off-flavors, however, come from excessively large growths of algae in the ponds, the most common being blue-green algae, which is the algae responsible for the occasional Mediterranean blue–colored pond. Although too much algae is bad, the presence of *some* algae in a pond is as important to growing fish as water, because these plants aerate the pond by manufacturing oxygen through photosynthesis while the sun is shining. They are nature's aerators, and there are always algae in a pond. In fact, there are algae almost everywhere. A glass of water left in the sunshine on a window sill will grow algae, to say nothing of a pond with thousands of gallons of water in it sitting out under the Delta sun. So blue-green algae occurs to some degree in most ponds, and its presence does not always mean that a fish will be off-flavor. However, in those ponds where there is too much of it, there is a possibility that some, or all, of the fish in that pond will not taste right. And there is no sure-fire method for controlling the algae. There are only a handful of chemicals approved for use in food-fish ponds, and while they include copper sulphate, which is occasionally effective in reducing algae growth, it is slow-acting and expensive.

Before a processing plant buys the contents of a pond, the fish are sampled three times: two weeks before they are harvested, then one

week before, and then the day before. In addition, the processing plants have the right to take a sample from a load of fish when it arrives, and send the whole load back to the pond if that one sample is off-flavor. Each processing plant hires a flavor checker to test the samples. The flavor checkers test samples of cooked catfish from each pond to be harvested with the most sophisticated equipment known: the human tongue. And of all the tongues in the Delta, the one widely acknowledged to be the best is the one in Stanley Marshall's mouth.

"The kind of off-flavor that comes from blue-green algae is a musty, woody taste. You can't miss it," Marshall told me. He is a short, blond-haired man with a trim moustache and a ready smile. He does the taste tests for Delta Pride, the world's largest processor of farm-raised catfish. Delta Pride, headquartered on the southern edge of Indianola off Highway 49, processed about $145 million worth of catfish in 1990, nearly 35 percent of the entire United States production. The company is cooperatively owned by about 180 farmer/shareholders, but despite the fact that each catfish farmer owns a piece of the company, no one gets any favoritism when it comes to taste-testing, according to both plant officials and farmers. Quality control is too important for everyone.

When a farmer has fish to sell to Delta Pride, a sample fish from each pond to be harvested is brought to Marshall. This is a job the catfish farmer usually does himself. Delta Pride keeps reserved parking places for farmers in back of the plant, next to a low, aluminum-sided building that houses the kitchen where Marshall works. When the farmer comes in with his fish, Stanley cuts the whole raw fish in half with big meat scissors, throws the front half— head and guts—into a big trash barrel, and puts the rear half in a small, brown paper sack, on which he writes the farmer's initials and the pond number. The bag is popped into a microwave for a few minutes. There are two microwaves on the kitchen counter cooking catfish all day long. Stanley estimates he probably tested over 300,000 samples of fish in 1990. Not all of those were taste samples,

by any means. He makes first-round choices with his nose. If a sample is off, it is likely to smell bad to him. If he is not quite sure, then he tastes it and makes his decision. Then, if the first samples from a pond pass, the pond is scheduled for harvest.

When Marshall says a fish is off-flavor, it is bad news for the catfish farmer, because there is not much to do except leave all the fish in the pond, keep spending money to feed them, and wait for them to come back "on-flavor." Often, this takes only a couple of weeks, but sometimes it takes months. The difference between on- and off-flavor is not so great as to be beyond dispute, however, and there are those farmers who feel Marshall is a little too zealous. When I was there, he gave me a taste test of two catfish—one on- and one off-flavor—and I could not tell the difference.

Understandably, Marshall's job can be a ticklish one. To tell a farmer that $50,000 worth of fish cannot be sold because their flavor is not quite right can earn a fellow an enemy. But this does not happen to Marshall. He is respected as an open, honest man, and, in addition, everyone agrees that, overzealous or not, there is no one better at tasting catfish. In 1988, when Stanley's wife, in her early thirties, became the second person in the country to undergo a successful double lung transplant, catfish farmers kicked in a substantial share of the costs not covered by insurance.

I heard a lot of Stanley Marshall stories. One is about a farmer who brought some samples in an ice chest in the back of his pickup, sitting next to his black Labrador Retriever. Black Labs are much admired in the Delta, and they are a common sight in the back of pickups. As the truck went over the railroad tracks that cross the road in front of the Delta Pride plant, the top of the ice chest was jarred loose. The farmer parked the truck at the plant and put the lid back on the chest, shooing away the Lab, which was licking one of the uncovered fish on its bed of ice. When Marshall brought the sample out of the microwave and sniffed it, he is said to have told the farmer, "Smells like dog's breath."

While I was watching Marshall work in the kitchen one morning,

a farmer came in with some fish to be sampled. As Stanley waited for the microwave's bell, he told us a story: "One guy had the fish spill out, and when he brought them in I told him it smelled like the bed of a pickup. You know that kind of oily, greasy smell on the floor of a pickup? There was another guy brought in a fish that he had tossed in a bucket where some empty beer cans had been. I told him the fish smelled like beer." The bell went off. Stanley took out the paper sack, set it on the Formica countertop, and tore it open, sticking his nose into the steam that billowed out through the tear in the bag. The farmer watched him with furrowed brow.

"Whew, man," Stanley exclaimed and wrinkled his nose. "Smells like diesel fuel."

Bang. That meant $50,000 had to stay out there in the pond, swimming around until God knew when. The farmer's face fell. "We did have a diesel spill in that pond one day," he admitted and shook his head. "I just wanted to know how bad it was."

"Well, give it a couple of weeks and bring one in," Stanley told him, and beckoned me over to smell the fish. Try as I might, I could not sense the faintest hint of diesel fuel. Maybe there was something not quite right about the smell, but to me it was nothing more than that. I would have happily wolfed it down had it been surrounded on a plate by hush puppies, fries, and coleslaw.

Each share of stock in Delta Pride represents an acre of catfish pond. In addition to being able to sell fish to the plant, a farmer/shareholder receives a cash dividend at the end of a profitable year. When Delta Pride was formed in 1981, a share of its stock sold for $55. In 1990, a share was valued at about $1,000. This kind of success did not go unnoticed, and Delta Pride soon had plenty of competitors. Most, like Delta Pride, were owned cooperatively by farmers.

A farmer whose fish is rejected by Stanley Marshall is perfectly free to take other samples from the same pond to be taste-tested at another plant. Perhaps the plant will have an order to fill and be in desperate need of fish, or perhaps the sample will pass the muster of

a less discriminating tongue than Stanley's. No one in the industry denies this happens, and that on occasion off-flavor fish reach the marketplace, but each plant rejects enough fish to make it unlikely that much poor product gets through. While farmers want to sell as many fish as possible, they also have a vested interest in not trying to circumvent the local quality control system. As farmers, they want the product to continue rising in acceptance, and as shareholders in a processing plant, they do not want their brand to get a bad name in the marketplace.

Delta Pride was the first processing plant to be cooperatively owned by farmers, and its formation in 1981 marked a turning point for the industry, a completion of its vertical integration. Now, there are hatcheries, ponds, feed mills, and processing plants, all owned by Delta farmers, all in accordance with the agricultural exemption from federal anti-trust laws. This vertical integration was the most important factor in the industry's success, according to Tommy Taylor, and he should know, if anyone does.

Tommy Taylor was the Humphreys County extension agent for thirty years, from 1959 to 1989. "Vertical integration is the thing that has stabilized this industry," he told me. "First came the feed mill—Producer's Feed opened in 1976—so the farmer could get the quantity and quality of feed he wanted. That was really critical, because the feed companies in other places were really putting it to us, both in price and quality. By the end of the first week that Producer's Feed was open, feed had dropped by fifty dollars a ton."

During Taylor's tenure as county agent, he nurtured the catfish industry like a parent does a child and was ready to serve catfish farmers in any way, at any hour. He put together the county's first catfish lab: a sink, six pails, and a microscope in an empty room behind his office on the top floor of the shadowy old Belzoni courthouse.

Taylor knows as much about the catfish industry as any man alive. He is a short man with a sizable paunch and an open countenance, an enthusiastic tobacco chewer. Any conversation with him is punctuated by frequent pauses to spit tobacco juice. His pickup truck has a cup-holder mounted on the dashboard with a paper cup in it, to which he had frequent recourse as he drove me around the county, giving me a tour of catfish country, pointing out various landmarks in the history of the Delta's aquaculture. We passed a huge spread of ponds, one of the largest in the world to belong to one family, he said. In another field, a bulldozer was going over the bottom of a drained pond, reshaping it before the pond was filled for another ten years. We covered lots of ground, from Isola in the north of Humphreys County to Silver City in the south. At one point we pulled off the road and watched some men harvesting a pond, tractors on levees across from each other, each pulling on one end of a huge seine net, moving slowly down the pond. "The first year we grew any catfish in this county was in 1966," Taylor said. "Just a couple hundred acres. I remember a farmer named J. B. Williams called me up with some problem, and I didn't know anything about catfish." But he soon learned.

Delta Pride's processing plant was not the first in the area, only the first cooperative. Three plants predated it, each built and owned by multinational corporations—Hormel, Con-Agra, and Prudential—and each of them was marketing catfish by the time Delta Pride was formed. Labor trouble closed Prudential's plant in 1985, but two of the three—Hormel and Con-Agra—were still up and running in 1990, together accounting for about 35 percent of the market. Taylor was not worried about the presence of outsiders in the industry, but he said it means that local farmers have to stand together to ensure that fish quality stays high.

"We're going to have more and more people from outside come in, because catfish look like they might be a real lucrative investment," he told me. "There's always the chance that if you get too much of that, quality could be affected. We've established a reputation for

quality, and if we lost that it wouldn't take long for us to go out of business.

"Right now, the farmer controls the feed, the fish, the processing, and the marketing, so there's already a pretty strong group here with its set way of doing things. As long as we have the control we have right now, we dictate quality, but if we lost our strength, if, say, something happened to Delta Pride's leadership position, an outside group could come in, take over, and screw up the whole thing."

One threat to Delta Pride's position, according to most industry observers, is the company's history of poor labor relations. Delta Pride was operating three plants in 1990—one in Humphreys County and two in Sunflower County. The main plant and company headquarters on the outskirts of Indianola was the town's largest employer, with a workforce of over 1,000, and overall the company had more than 1,800 employees. The management team, hired by the farmer/shareholders to run the processing plant, was adamantly antiunion, although Delta Pride's workforce was successfully organized by the United Food and Commercial Workers in 1987 and won a three-year contract. When that contract expired, in August 1990, a bitter four-month strike followed, during which there were the beginnings of a nationwide boycott of Delta Pride products. A contract was finally signed, in line with other union contracts at other processing plants in the Delta, but only after a lot of bitterness between management and labor. Even then, the contract left most people at the plants working for close to minimum wage with a poor medical benefits program. Conditions are not great in any of the plants, even those where workers consider themselves well treated.

Up until the 1950s, when all the farms mechanized and sharecropping ceased to be a way of life, poor people in the Delta grew up working in the fields, chopping cotton, which means chopping

out the weeds growing in the rows and around the plants with a hoe. Many of the people I talked to who worked at catfish processing plants, particularly those who worked at Delta Pride, said the only difference between chopping catfish and chopping cotton was being indoors under a roof rather than outdoors under the brutal Delta sun. The work in a catfish plant is tedious and repetitive, whether it is processing the fish as they arrive on a conveyor belt—beheading, gutting, and skinning them—or standing around a cutting table on a wet cement floor, cutting the fish into filet strips with a razor-sharp filet knife. Whatever the job, there is always a quota to be met, a certain number of pounds to be done each hour, and constant work is required to meet it.

The workers who perform these jobs are almost all black women. There are some men hired to drive forklifts and shovel ice to pack the fish in, but the plants generally hire from the Delta's most under-utilized labor pool—young, black women—much the same as the farmers put ponds in their most under-utilized land. While working conditions in 1990 were mediocre at best and the pay low, plant officials were quick to point out that work was being provided for a segment of the population that would otherwise be on public assistance. For that segment of the black population that would not, otherwise, have been on public assistance, for the working men and women of the Delta's black communities, the processing plants were of little assistance. There was only one black-owned catfish processing plant in the state, and there were probably less than half a dozen black people in any kind of management position at a plant. This, despite the fact that it was African-American catfish consumers who carried the industry through its lean years and kept it afloat.

That irony did not escape Ron Myers, and he was determined to do something about it. The thirty-four-year-old black physician threatened in 1990 to organize one thousand black marchers to protest and boycott the World Catfish Festival to protest the fact that Belzoni was spending $30,000 on the festival and not doing enough for its poorest citizens. Boycotts and marches were serious weapons

in the Delta, used sparingly, but sometimes with great effectiveness, and the organizers of the festival were not happy to hear someone talking about a boycott and the catfish festival in the same breath. It would have severely thinned the numbers of folks looking and buying at the booths of the festival's flea market and consuming barbecue on the lawn in front of the courthouse.

The Belzoni-Humphreys County Industrial Development Board was one of the power-brokering bodies in the county, and while 70 percent of Humphreys County was black, ten of the eleven board members were white. Myers was demanding a regular dialogue with board members to assure that black citizens and their needs were not left out of county plans for development.

"Issues like education, community development, one of the highest infant mortality rates in the country, and health care need to be addressed so that we can go forward and make our area more attractive for industry," he told me. "If the black community is not included in the dialogue and not part of the plans, it won't work. It's not just a black-white issue really, it's rich and poor, because poor whites suffer a lot in the Delta, too."

He knew because he treated many of them while on duty in the emergency room at the Humphreys County Hospital in Belzoni. Myers first came to Belzoni in 1987 to work at a clinic in order to repay the National Health Service Corps for his medical education at the University of Wisconsin. In hindsight, the white people of Belzoni would probably have been willing to pay it for him in order to keep him out of town.

Myers recalls that at medical school, his professors were always chiding him for his political activities, telling him to pay attention to his education and leave protests to others. He never did. When he graduated, he did his residency in Bogalusa, Louisiana, where he met and married Sylvia Holmes, who shared his activist streak. After he completed his residency, they came to Belzoni, where he quickly became involved in local civil rights issues. In 1990, he was vice president of the county's NAACP branch. In addition to prac-

ticing medicine, Myers is a Baptist preacher and a jazz pianist. He has a small congregation in Belzoni and spends an occasional Saturday night in Jackson, jamming with other jazz musicians, then driving the ninety miles back home in time to rest and get up the next morning to preach.

In 1989, Myers decided to begin a small clinic in Tchula, twenty miles east of Belzoni, a nearly all-black town that had no doctor. When the National Health Service Corps balked at allowing him to leave Belzoni for Tchula, he used the media skills he had learned at Wisconsin, and before long the case of the doctor being forbidden to open a clinic in this desperately poor little town was in the *New York Times* and on network news. The Health Service relented, and Myers opened his clinic in Tchula.

Even before I called him up and went to visit, I had seen Myers on the local evening news and heard him talking about his struggle to gain access to the industrial development board and the possibility of a protest march during the catfish festival. He had already filed a request for a march permit with the Belzoni police department. He sounded serious, and people were taking him that way, but a week before the festival, the board finally agreed to meet with Myers and begin working out a mechanism for giving Belzoni's poorest citizens some input to the board.

One day, before that happened, I was visiting a white catfish farmer in Humphreys County, and he told me a story about Myers. He said that the day before, Myers was driving from Belzoni to Tchula when he stopped in at the feed store to get something and "some of the boys there beat the shit out of him. He'll be singing a different tune today, you bet."

When I asked Myers himself about getting beaten up in the feed store, he laughed heartily. He had heard stories like that before, but had never actually been physically attacked. There is enough of him that it was easy to see why. He is a large, pear-shaped man, built big and bearish by nature, and even bigger due to being considerably overweight. He parked me in his small office with a folder of news-

paper clippings about himself and the clinic, while he saw patients in one of two examining rooms. His wife, Sylvia, who is the receptionist, bookkeeper, and general assistant, was in an office by a small waiting room, and their young son Joshua wandered back and forth from me to his mother to the doorway of the tiny room not much longer than the examining table inside where his father was working, until Myers looked up and shooed him back to the waiting room, where he would begin his toddling peregrinations all over again.

Myers talked to me between patients. "We have an infant mortality in this county of thirty-four percent, three times the national average, in a country that is ranked twenty-eighth in the world to begin with," he said, bitterness in his voice. "And the flus and colds and pneumonia I see during the winter I couldn't begin to tell you about. People have inadequate housing, and they get a cold, and it just goes on into pneumonia. The amount of pneumonia I see in the winter is pathetic. Look at the houses. They have no insulation and are poorly built. One kid gets sick and they all get sick."

When he was finished with his patients, he joined me in the office and ate his lunch, which someone had brought from down the road: a huge slab of fried fish slathered with hot sauce between two pieces of white bread, and an orange soda. More patients would be in soon, so he ate and talked about catfish at the same time. "You're talking about ninety-nine percent black folks chopping the catfish, the plants reaping profits of millions of dollars from the Delta, and where is the return to the community? We want to see some of those dollars that are in the catfish industry. We'd like to see more opportunities open up in the area of management for blacks. We're encouraging them to put together a summer management internship program for some of the brighter high school students. We'd like to see community centers and better health care for the workers."

He took a bite of his sandwich, which smelled spicy and delicious. "Blacks were locked out of either farming or processing catfish from the beginning. The industry does not have any opportunity for

blacks except chopping the catfish. What happens to our talented kids when they grow up and go off to college? We want some opportunities for them in management. It is time to approach the industry about this."

We talked a long time, then some more patients came in and I hung around the front office to talk Cajun cooking with Sylvia and play with Joshua. It was twilight when I left the clinic and drove out of Tchula back to Indianola. People stood in dusky shadows along the road, talking and laughing. A few miles outside of town, in a deep afternoon light with the sun low on the horizon, was a small, one-room church with a broad porch and a cross perched on the roof. The building was at the edge of a ploughed field, which ran right up to the church's back wall. On one side of the church was a small cemetery, a rectangular plot of tended ground with four rows of well-weathered and worn tombstones. The fields around it were green with knee-high cotton.

CHAPTER IV

Big and Little Catfish

I HAD packed two rods in the van with me when I went to the Delta: one with an open-faced spinning reel on it, the other with a new bait-casting reel my father had recently given me. I had tried casting with it in the backyard before I left, and the line sailed out effortlessly in a graceful arc, settling gently on the grass. I was eager to get it wet.

One Saturday morning I drove down from Indianola to Belzoni to interview ex-county agent Tommy Taylor at his home. We talked about all the ways a farmer can lose money growing catfish, the numerous things that can go wrong in a pond. He estimated that a

well-managed pond had a mortality rate of about 8 percent each year, and told me that even while losing a few thousand fish, a farmer could still expect a net profit of $500 to $1,000 an acre at harvest time.

During our talk, Taylor's wife, Betty, and their tow-headed grandson came home from a trip to the hardware store for fishing tackle. It turned out that she and Taylor were planning to take the boy fishing in a catfish pond later in the morning. I wheedled, cajoled, and did everything short of beg for an invitation. "Let him come, Papaw," the boy seconded my request, and I was included.

I followed the Taylor family's truck, and we drove for a long way, the last three or four miles on a dirt road, far back in the cotton fields to a group of ponds gleaming under the sun and blue sky. Up on the levee, Taylor's thirty-year-old son was waiting for us—it turned out I had horned in on more of a family outing than I had realized.

Tommy Taylor has a relentless sense of humor. Short and rotund, he likes to keep people off-balance and laughing. He has done hundreds of interviews with print and television journalists writing pieces on the Delta's catfish industry. For better than twenty-five years, reporters have found their way to him, along with just about anyone else who is curious about the catfish industry. He has led Americans, Africans, Asians, and Europeans through the Delta, and touted catfish to anyone who would listen, in addition to having served as a dedicated and effective county agent.

While we stood at the back of his pickup, passing around a plastic container of raw chicken livers and baiting our hooks with them, Taylor kept up a running patter. "Folks all over the world are pretty much the same," he mused. "Me and my wife have gotten around quite a bit. The first time we did any traveling, we had a flat tire right outside of Clarksdale, and I learned right away folks anywhere are the same: people all stopped their cars and while no one actually helped me change the tire, they all stood around and offered advice. Just like home. . . ."

The chicken liver was slimy as I picked it out of its bath of watery blood, and it had the smell of raw organ. I threaded the hook through its meatiest part and wondered if it would stay on when I cast it out, or whether I would have to repeat the process after my first cast.

"Don't worry, that'll stay on good," said Taylor, reading my mind. "Say, did you hear about the guy who died and went to heaven? When he got there, Saint Peter told him he had to marry to get in, and brought him the ugliest woman you might ever hope to see. 'How come such an ugly woman?' the guy asked, and Saint Pete told him, 'You've got to pay for your sins on earth.'

"Then the guy sees me sitting on a cloud inside the pearly gates with a harp and a beautiful woman. A Miss America type. 'How come Tommy Taylor got such a beautiful woman?' he asked. 'She's got to pay for her sins, too,' said Saint Pete."

What he did not tell me while we baited our hooks and laughed was that we would not be catching normal, market-size one-and-a-half-pound catfish in this pond, but were much more likely to tie into some ten-pound fish. He did give me one piece of advice: when the bobber went under I should wait a second and set the hook.

My first cast was everything I had hoped for, a long, gliding, silken arc, and my red and white float rode the water farther out than anyone else's. "Nice cast," Taylor said, and my heart swelled with the pride that goeth before a fall.

Almost immediately, the round white plastic of the float was jerked under, and disappeared beneath the surface. I yanked the pole back to set the hook, and a moment later the catfish out there in the middle of the pond yanked back. I was unprepared for the strength of it, loosely holding the rod and reel, which jumped out of my hands and into the pond in a heartbeat. I started to wade in after it, but after my first step I knew it was too late. I saw a flash of rod and reel, underwater, being quickly towed by a large fish to the center of the pond, and in a moment it was gone. There was no sense

diving in to chase it, and little chance the earth was about to open beneath my feet and swallow me, although that was what I would have preferred to facing the Taylor family, witnesses to the dumbest thing I had done in a lifetime of fishing.

"I guess they must have a different kind of catfish where you come from, huh?" Taylor asked, almost able to keep a straight face. I still had one rod, but my own face was on fire, and I could not bear the thought of remaining there with the Taylors for another second. I mumbled something about an upcoming appointment, got in my van, and fled, imagining mocking laughter trailing me for the whole hour's drive back to Indianola.

Fortunately, I got a second opportunity to fish that pond six weeks later. I was better prepared for what I would find there, and spent the day horsing ten-pound catfish to the bank. While I was grateful that the big fish were still in there, Jack Reed, the owner of the pond, was not happy about it at all. Those fish were costing him money and had been for a long time.

Once a fish hits one and a half pounds, you can cut a pair of filet-size portions for a restaurant or a supermarket seafood counter from its flanks. But that is the limit. Even if it gets a few pounds bigger, you can still only get the same portion from each side of the fish. Filets are what the processing plants like to do, since they wholesale for more money than the other forms the fish is sold in: strips, nuggets, or whole. Plants do not want big fish because they cost more to buy since they weigh more, but they do not yield more filets for the market. There is some demand in the live seafood markets of big cities for large, whole catfish, but not much, and none of the plants wanted Reed's ten-pounders. He had no choice but to keep the fish alive and wait for one of the periodic shortages of catfish to affect the plants, so that they would buy anything they could get.

Reed farmed fourteen ponds—187 acres of water. "I got caught with a lot of big fish. Two of those ponds were off-flavor all year long for two years, and the fish just got big. After three or four years with

a pond, you'll always have a few big ones that don't get seined, but I had a build-up and they just kept growing, and the first thing I knew I was sitting here with a bunch of big catfish.

"Two years ago fish got short, and I should have gone in there and then and seined those ponds out, cleaned them out and sold everything, but I didn't do it, because I had a contract with a processor and thought I'd need the fish to sell there further down the road. I didn't really know how many I had in there. Then I started getting caught with off-flavor and there they are. You go ahead and fish those ponds whenever you want, that'll be a few less I have to feed."

Reed grew up where he still lives, in the tiny town of Silver City, and he grows fish on the land where his forefathers grew cotton. Silver City is made up of a couple of general stores and a juke joint at a crossroads a few miles south of Belzoni, but, small as it is, some quite prosperous white farmers live there. Reed went to the University of Mississippi, where he starred in both baseball and football, went into the service for two years, and, when he got out in 1960, signed a contract with the New York Yankee baseball organization as an outfielder. He played a year in the minor leagues, then went up to the Yankees in 1961 as the second-string center fielder behind Mickey Mantle and sat on the bench for three of the team's best years in its history. The Yankees were in the World Series each of the three seasons he was with them, and they won two out of the three. Reed was wearing a World Series ring when I met him. The Mick, however, did not miss a lot of games, and Reed, during three years in the major leagues, only came up to bat about two hundred times. He is tall, sandy-haired, and when I met him he still had the rugged jaw of a good center fielder. Reed quit playing in 1964, but he stayed in the Yankee organization, first as a coach, then as a minor league manager in Binghampton, New York. In 1968, his father died, and he came home to take over the family farm.

In the long run, catfish had been good to him, but things had gotten tighter over the past couple of years. "There's just not a whole lot you can do when those fish come up off-flavor," he said. "I'll tell

you how to get rich: come up with something that'll get fish back on-flavor. It has caused me a lot of worry with these ponds full of big fish. The live-haulers will take some of them and carry them to places like Baton Rouge. Fish are getting a little short again, so maybe I'll get rid of them yet. The thing was, there were a lot more in there than I thought. That was the problem. There's just no way to know how many's in there. You can keep all the records you want to, use a computer and everything, but I'm telling you there's still no way to know how many fish you've got in there."

Of course, a farmer knows how many fingerlings, more or less, were originally stocked in a pond, but it is easy to lose track as time goes on, even though catfish will not breed in a pond because it lacks the requisite privacy and dark holes where they like to spawn. Fish in a pond get harvested and sold, more are put in to replace them, more get sold, some die, another batch is added, and it becomes increasingly difficult to say with assurance how many fish are in a given pond. This was why Delta banks stopped taking fish in the pond as collateral on loans to catfish farmers. It was also why a senior scientist at the University of Mississippi's National Center for Physical Acoustics is working on a project to use sonar to image the fish in a pond and count them precisely. If that could be done, the hope is that banks would look more favorably on catfish as assets.

The other method for persuading banks to soften their stance would be a big growth in the industry, and industry observers say that could best be achieved by getting catfish on the fast-food menus. Catfish fries well and could easily be adapted to fast food, if the production levels were kept up and the price held down.

But even if it becomes possible to take a sonar picture showing how many fish are actually in a pond, and the market could handle as many fish as could be grown, catfish would still be something less than rock-steady collateral. There are too many things that can hap-

pen to a fish before it gets sold. The worst, of course—even worse than off-flavor—is death, which comes sneaking into ponds by a number of routes. A pond full of fish one day can be a pond full of unmarketable dead meat the next, and there are a lot of ways for that to happen, including diseases, low oxygen, predatory birds, and parasites.

Catfish farming is like any other kind of farming in this sense. As soon as you cultivate a formerly wild species, be it flora or fauna, as soon as you attempt to control its environment, grow it, and harvest it in quantity, nature seems to oppose you, constantly injecting chaos into the order you are trying to create. A species may be domesticated only so long as there is a farmer who is willing to struggle endlessly with natural calamities in order to grow it.

One such calamity in the Delta is the double-breasted cormorant, a bird most catfish farmers had never heard of in 1980. For centuries, the Delta was nothing more than a fly-over for these birds, in a long route extending from their breeding grounds and summer home in Canada to their winter residence along the Gulf Coast of Louisiana. For decades, the Delta's endless fields of cotton did not catch their attention. As the catfish industry prospered, however, and the number of ponds increased, many cormorants took to settling down for a winter's roost in the Delta. For a cormorant, one of the most skillful of all avian fishers, feeding itself from a catfish pond is like shooting fish in a barrel. The birds spend their days on the surface and eat whenever the urge strikes them. A single cormorant can eat a pound of fish a day, and a flock of them can pretty well devour the fifty thousand fish in a pond over the course of a winter. At night they roost, but during winter days a farmer is constantly at risk of serious loss to these catfish-eating birds.

The usual response of a Delta farmer to this kind of nuisance would be to take his gun out of the rack, load up on shells, and start shooting. However, cormorants are a federally-protected species of migratory bird, and the fine for killing just one is $10,000. Besides which, they are hard to hit: their dark bodies ride low on the surface

of the ponds, their long necks and hooked beaks about all of the target that shows. The only legal way to deal with a cormorant invasion is to scare them off the ponds, and a wide range of strategies have been developed with that end in mind: propane-fired cannons that erupt at irregular intervals with a great roar of noise, which rolls across the fields; whooping sirens; hired hands who drive around the levees in pickups firing guns into the air. Farmers can also file for a depredation permit, which allows them to kill twenty-five cormorants each year. Other popular methods of scaring off cormorants include building scarecrows on the pond banks and leaving cars on the levee with their hoods up, which many consider the most effective, although no one is sure why. Nothing works for long, however, even if some things work sometimes, and nothing does more than scare the birds over to a neighbor's pond, from which they will eventually be scared back.

Another ever-present threat is disease, something that threatens all farmers, whether they produce vegetables, fruit, or meat. When fifty thousand catfish are put in a ten-acre pond, eating and excreting, they become vulnerable to a number of diseases, most of which are named and identifiable, but not all of which are understood or responsive to treatment. Some occur only during particular times of the year, while others are ever-present. They include viral, bacterial, and parasitical diseases. For some there are antidotes, but for others the only thing to do is wait for the disease to run its course and hope that the mortality rate stays low.

The number of legal remedies for diseases is severely limited. In 1990, only two antibiotics were approved by the United States Food and Drug Administration for introduction into a pond where catfish are being raised for human consumption. A sulfanomide called RO-5 was approved in 1984, but is rarely used due to its high cost and the lack of data supporting its effectiveness. The other approved antibiotic is Terramycin, an old standby in the antibiotic pharmacopeia. It has been approved since the beginnings of catfish farming and is occasionally effective against bacterial diseases like colum-

naris and edwardsiella, both of which can prove fatal to large numbers of fish. In the case of a brood fish pond at a hatchery, where fish are being kept for reproductive purposes, it is sometimes actually feasible to inject individual fish with Terramycin, but for the farmer who is raising food fish, the idea of injecting fifty thousand fish is unthinkable. The only way to get antibiotics into fish is by using medicated feed.

A ton of feed in which each pellet carries a dose of Terramycin costs about twice as much to buy as an unmedicated ton. If a ton of standard 32-percent-protein feed was selling for $250, the same feed, medicated, goes for about $500. A ton of feed medicated with RO-5 might be three times as high as unmedicated feed. Most farmers feel that if either antibiotic could be counted on to work consistently it would be worth the price, but fish often stop eating when they get sick, and the medicated feed sometimes proves to be too little, too late.

This was a lesson that had to be learned. There was a period during the late 1970s when farmers began to use medicated feed as a prophylactic measure. They were willing to pay the higher price for protection, and they gave their healthy fish regular doses of Terramycin in the hope it would prevent the appearance of bacterial diseases. In addition, as soon as they noticed a few dead fish in their ponds, they would switch to medicated feed before they had ascertained whether it was a bacterial disease doing the killing.

By 1980, an alarming trend of drug resistance became apparent. That year, over 50 percent of the bacteria isolated from sick catfish in the laboratories of Mississippi State University's cooperative extension service were drug-resistant. The catfish division of the extension service has offices and laboratories at the Delta Branch Experimental Station, located at Stoneville, twenty miles west of Indianola. Because they are surrounded by catfish farmers and into some cooperatively financed research projects with the catfish industry, the extension service agents are not in the habit of making proclamations. They see a lot of money being spent and made, so

they stick to research and stay out of setting policy. But in September 1980, the extension service issued a warning in a bulletin sent to catfish farmers, in which they detailed the results of their laboratory tests and strongly advised farmers to use medicated feed only if bacterial disease was present in a pond.

While feed for cows, pigs, and chickens is routinely medicated, it is not now in the catfish industry, and this is to the benefit of those who consume the fish. Studies, such as those detailed in Orville Schell's book, *Modern Meat*, show that meat produced on a modern American farm where feed is routinely medicated can pass along an antibiotic resistance to the human who eats it—resistance to the very antibiotics, like Terramycin, that might one day be needed by that person to fight disease. Despite entrenched resistance from the pharmaceutical companies that manufacture the medication and the livestock farmers who have become dependent on antibiotics to replace the techniques of good husbandry, it appears likely that regulations prohibiting the use of medicated feed for anything but the treatment of very specific, temporary conditions will be put in place eventually. In fact, the European community had already enacted such regulations by 1990.

When those rules do come along for this country, they will not disturb catfish farmers. "I was using that medicated feed for a bunch of years," one manager of an Isola catfish farm told me in a contemptuous voice. "Then they told us it didn't do a damned bit of good and they were right. What's more, fish are just like you and me—they lose their appetite when they get sick, and you can't get enough feed in 'em to make a difference."

Mississippi State's extension service, which issued that early warning about antibiotic resistance, is, not surprisingly, the nation's leading academic research institution in the field of catfish aquaculture. There are more than sixty ponds and five full-time researchers at the Delta Branch facility.

"Because of the unique situation here, where the extension service works directly with both the researchers and the farmers, we have a

good flow of information both ways," said Randy MacMillan, a fisheries specialist at the station. "Research is directly delivered to the catfish farmer, and his problems are prioritized and given to the researchers to work on."

MacMillan was a marine biologist from the Pacific Northwest, who had done his doctoral work at the University of Washington, where salmon are farmed. Three years in Stoneville had turned him into a catfish man. Young, clean-cut, and earnest, he got excited when he talked about catfish.

"What we do here is try to translate our work into practical benefits for the farmer," MacMillan said. "Our knowledge is growing, but at the same time there's always something unexpected to deal with, or something we expect, but still don't know how to deal with."

One of the diseases in the "expected" category is the one farmers call "winter kill." Every winter, millions of catfish die in the ponds for no apparent reason. Year in and year out, winter kill accounts for losses of over $20 million to Delta catfish farmers. There appears to be no rhyme or reason as to why fish in one pond die and those in another remain healthy through the winter.

Another disease that can come as a nasty surprise is known as "hamburger gill." Farmers call it that because affected fish develop gills that look like chopped beef: mushy, undefined masses of meat, rather than the feathery, finely etched gills of a healthy fish. Hamburger gill is the severe emphysema of the catfish world. An afflicted fish gets less and less water through its gills as the disease progresses, and it suffocates in a matter of days. Not only is there no known cure, but researchers are still not even sure what causes it. What everyone does know is that it can spread rapidly and wipe out an entire pond. Catfish farmers who have experienced an outbreak speak of it like the plague—a scourge of unknown origin that can appear at any time. The one saving grace about hamburger gill is that it does not affect the meat while the fish is still alive, so if the disease is recognized early in a pond, a farmer can harvest and sell as many fish

as he can find a plant to buy. This depends on a rapid diagnosis of the condition so flavor samples can be taken and a pond harvested before all its inhabitants suffocate.

One morning, when I was talking to MacMillan, he got a call from a worried farmer in Isola, who thought the fish in one of his ponds might have hamburger gill. He went out to look at the pond, and I rode with him. Driving in a small pickup with the university's logo on the door, we took an hour to get there, which MacMillan said was the average distance for one of his house calls. We drove beside vast tracts of farmland, the eight-row cultivators looking small across the distance as they went up and down the fields, insignificant clouds of dust in the air behind them, far across the panorama.

Our destination lay down a long and dusty dirt road outside Isola. MacMillan drove straight to the pond without first looking for the farmer. He knew the farm and had been there before, as he had to many of the farms in Sunflower and Humphreys counties. We drove up on the levee. The pond lay placidly under the sunshine, turtles on the banks, startled by our arrival, jumping into the water with a wet plop. Big dragonflies skimmed the surface, sunlight making rainbows of their translucent wings, and an abundance of red-winged blackbirds was in the air. But the water in the pond held a different story: It was like a walled city in a plague-ridden country seen from a distance, seemingly undisturbed and tranquil until its walls were breached to reveal corpses rotting in the streets. Mac-Millan stopped the truck and got out, cautioning me to leave my door open when I followed him.

"Catfish have exceptionally good hearing," he told me, *sotto voce*. "If you close a truck door, every catfish around will head for the bottom."

We stepped gingerly across the levee, and when we came to the bank of the pond, we saw some fish that would not have gone anywhere had we set off dynamite. The water's edge was dotted with fish floating in the shadows, white bellies up. MacMillan whispered, "When you start to see this many dead fish in a pond, you know

you've got a real problem. That's when you've got no time to lose. What's for sure, from what you can see right here, is that this guy's got trouble. Now we have to see what kind of trouble it is."

He tiptoed back to his truck and got a long-handled dip net from its bed. He had an ice chest packed with ice back there too, where he could keep samples from the pond alive until he got back to the lab in Stoneville. He pointed out a fish, just under the surface near the edge of the bank, with its snout and whiskers almost breaking water.

"That fish is almost dead," he said. "It's desperately looking for oxygen, which means that it's in the last stages of whatever is killing these others."

He dipped it up. The fish, a big fourteen or fifteen inches, appeared comatose. MacMillan held the fish with one hand and peeled back its gill cover with the other to reveal an undifferentiated mass of red gill. "This is a classic case of terminal hamburger gill."

Suddenly, a surge of life passed through the fish, which arched its body and spiked MacMillan with its dorsal spine. "Gosh darn it," he exclaimed, in the closest thing to profanity I'd heard him use. "That's one of the hazards of this job. I've gotten flat tires from running over the fins of dead catfish that the farmers have tossed up on the levee. Getting finned doesn't just hurt, it can give you fish monger's disease, which attacks muscle bundles and can actually be life-threatening. I should really carry a first-aid kit in the truck," he muttered, as he eyed the blood oozing from a puncture in the meat of his palm, below the thumb.

For all his work out at the ponds, MacMillan was still, basically, an academic, or he would have known what to do next in order to prevent swelling and pain. Every farmer and farm worker who has ever had anything to do with catfish knows that if you are stuck and

bleed, the thing to do is rub a little catfish slime—the mucuslike substance that coats the catfish skin—on the wound. The slime on a channel catfish is thickest down by the belly, and it is usually a catfish's stomach that is rubbed on a wound. Pain and inflammation disappear. This folk remedy has been given scientific credibility. Scientists from Kuwait and the United States reported in 1988 that experiments with an Arabian saltwater catfish demonstrated catfish slime to have as many as sixty different proteins that are healing agents, according to a biochemistry professor, Richard Criddle, from the University of California at Davis.

In the case of a catfish spiking that does not bleed—indicating that the spine has broken off inside the wound—catfish slime is not going to do much good. There are a number of options, none of which is all that great, ranging from strong antibiotics, to surgery, to wishing you were dead.

As anyone knows who has had it happen, getting stuck by a catfish is not like being finned by other species of fish. It can be much more than merely a sharp painful prick that passes quickly. The spines at the top of a catfish's dorsal and pectoral fins each have a venom gland by them, and when a catfish strikes, the gland's secretions can put a human being in some pretty bad pain for anywhere from twenty minutes to a couple of days. A catfish can bring its spine erect and lock it into place as fast as we can blink. Those are the spines that have punctured the tires on Randy MacMillan's pickup. If one of them breaks off in a hand or a foot, look out. In addition to delivering a load of venom to the wound, a spine can carry everything from hepatitis to tuberculosis, depending on what was in the water where the catfish has been swimming. In the case of wild catfish, that often means a river near a city, contaminated with raw, untreated sewage. An embedded catfish spine is often cause for hospitalization and an intravenous course of antibiotics, as well as minor surgery to remove it.

"If you get stuck and it bleeds, you're all right, but mister, if it

doesn't bleed, look out," a black farm worker named Victor Taylor told me. It was a Sunday morning, and I had taken my thirteen-year-old son, Emanuele, who was visiting Indianola for the weekend, down to Silver City and up on the levee of Jack Reed's pond. Taylor saw us from his house across the dirt road, and drove his battered pickup over to check on who was fishing in "Mister Jack's" pond.

"Jes' call me Taylor," he introduced himself. He said he had been working for the Reed family and living on their land for all sixty-four years of his life. He was dressed in a khaki cotton work shirt and old jeans, and he had dark brown skin with short, thinning, grey hair curled tightly to his scalp. His hands were big, his palms overlaid with pads of calluses that I felt when I shook his hand. He had only a pair of yellowed snaggle-teeth left in his mouth, one up and one down. Taylor sat behind the wheel in the truck with the door open, one beat-up athletic shoe stretched out and resting on the running board. I stood and leaned my back against the side of the truck bed in the bright sunshine, listening to him tell stories while Emanuele fished with his float bobbing in the small waves of the gleaming pond, calling us every so often to admire a ten-pounder dragged flopping up on the bank. He would work the hook out with pliers and nudge the fish with his shoe. It would slide flipping and flopping back down the bank and into the pond.

The sun shone down, and Taylor talked. Storytelling is a favorite pastime for people in the Delta, and they are wonderful at it. What might be the most common and boring anecdote elsewhere is fascinating if a Deltan is recounting it. Black or white, rich or poor, country or town dweller, everyone can tell a good story, lingering in just the right places to keep a hold on the listener's attention. It is a rare talent and something that flows from them naturally. Deltans also have a reputation for not letting a strict interpretation of the truth ruin a good story. Many of Taylor's tales that morning were about encounters with snakes. The ponds attract frogs, he said, and they, in turn, bring snakes. They include the common brown water

snakes, chicken snakes, and green snakes—"that bite'll make you sick"—and the more venomous water moccasins and rattlesnakes.

"There goes a brown snake now," he said, pointing toward the pond, a head barely visible above the water, leaving a tiny V-wake behind it as it glided. "Mister, I'm telling you, I'd just about rather get bit by a snake than get a fin stuck in me. If that catfish spike breaks off in your hand, your whole arm goes numb. If it breaks off in your foot, you can't feel a thing in your leg. If you get stuck like that, and you're by yourself, don't try to drive to the doctor. No sir. 'Cause you won't make it. Just lay down and wait for it to pass to where you can drive."

Little did I know on my embarrassing first visit to Jack Reed's pond with Tommy Taylor's family how lucky I had been. Once I began learning about catfish, I was grateful that the fish had not pulled me in behind the rod and reel. Both fact and folklore abound with ways in which catfish wreak some pretty terrible damage on human beings.

A poet named James Autry, who grew up in the Delta, remembers his father and friends going out "grabblin'": catching catfish by hand, wading chest-high through the backwaters of a river searching for big catfish holed up under logs. His father told him a story about a man who found a big one, and, reaching down to get it, inadvertently put his hand through the fish's mouth and got it caught up in the gills. The man's hand was stuck, and the fish began to drag him under the water. His companions seized his legs and tried to pull him up, and they had to struggle for the man in a tug-of-war with the fish before he worked his hand loose and was pulled free.

Size is no indication of a catfish's ferocity. There is a European catfish that grows as long as six feet, and people come from all over the world to fish for it. There is also a species of Amazonian catfish only three inches long and as big around as a shoelace, called the *candiru*. It is a parasitic catfish, attracted to the smell of urine, and it will enter the penis of a swimmer or wader and lodge in the urethra. Its residence there is so tenacious and painful that its victims are re-

puted to beg for amputation, and a milder form of surgery may actually be necessary. The Indians who live along these stretches of the Amazon wear penis sheaths when they go in the water.

In folktales, the catfish is an implacable foe. There are stories of catfish eating just about anything that falls in the water, from dogs to babies. Catfish are creatures from the dark side, and have never been friendly toward human beings. They have a lot in common with snapping turtles: both are surviving aquatic species from prehistory, both can do some pretty terrible damage to people when disturbed, particularly the big ones, and both can live in the wild to an old age and immense bulk. Channel catfish forty years old and weighing nearly sixty pounds have been recorded.

Of course, at a year old, and one and a half pounds, the channel catfish is considerably more controllable. In fact, the wholesale slaughter of so many millions of catfish before they even pass through their adolescence could be seen as the latest move by Homo sapiens to gain ascendancy in an age-old struggle. Even at a pound and a half, a catfish is never something to take lightly, and one way or another farm-raised fish have managed to leave scars on a sizeable number of the men and women who work in the industry, whether from finnings in the field or filet-knife cuts in the plant.

CHAPTER V

Running the Cans

The railroad divides the town roughly according to color. 'Across the Tracks' is used as the name of the Negro district, a label with obvious implications. Across the Tracks is a life but little known to the Whites, who rarely go there. Everything that happens on the whites' side, however, is known to the Negroes, who have constant access to white homes and business places.

Powdermaker, *After Freedom*

FROM HIGHWAY 82 on the northern edge of Indianola, it takes about three minutes to drive through the broad and shaded streets of the staid, white residential neighborhoods until you reach downtown,

with the two-story, brick Sunflower County courthouse, and the one-story buildings along Main Street. This was for many years the retail center of Indianola, although the discount stores and fast-food joints have pulled a lot of traffic out to Highway 82. The downtown has a Piggly-Wiggly supermarket, smaller and older than the supermarket out on the highway. Many of the town's poorer black people still take their business to the downtown Piggly-Wiggly—it is conveniently located, and they are welcomed and well treated there. The store also cashes welfare and family assistance checks. On certain afternoons, when the federal checks arrive in the mail, there is a line out into the parking lot of people clutching bureaucracy-brown envelopes. Many buy groceries before they leave. In 1986, the black citizens of Indianola boycotted downtown businesses for thirty-five days during a controversy over who would be superintendent of public schools, and the Piggly-Wiggly was the only business exempted.

Farther along the sidewalk from the supermarket are three clothing stores, each owned by a Jewish family; a hardware store; a cafe; a pawn shop; a video rental store run by a southeast Asian couple; and a drugstore. At the southern end of Main Street are railroad tracks. It takes another three minutes to cross them and drive through the less staid and rich, but equally residential, neighborhoods of black Indianola. The town dribbles out into the country, the houses growing littler, shabbier, and farther apart, and then there is nothing but open fields planted in cotton and beans.

Far clearer than this dividing line between town and country is the one separating white and black Indianola. The handful of streets that cross the tracks and go through black Indianola to the countryside pass through older, somewhat rundown neighborhoods, and these streets are the only part of black Indianola most white residents ever see. They rarely, if ever, pass through the streets of neat homes surrounded by yards in the newer black subdivisions, because they are mostly dead-ends, not streets to travel through on the way to anywhere. There is a black middle class in Indianola, small

but doing well, made up primarily of public workers, attorneys, doctors, preachers, and teachers. White Indianolans rarely meet these people. They have limited their encounters with black people to those with whom they have an employer/employee relationship, whether it be a housewife and her domestic, or a farmer and his tractor driver.

The truth is, white Indianolans would probably feel right at home in many of the town's black neighborhoods. The houses might be a little smaller than their own, but they would recognize the terrain as familiar: the same comfortable chairs and sofa grouped around a big television set and VCR, the same knick-knacks on dusted tables, clean towels in the bathroom, yards trimmed with Weed-eaters. They would also be right at home with the do-what-you-want-on-Saturday-night-but-be-in-church-Sunday-morning ethic. Work hard during the week, then fish, hunt, and socialize on the weekend—this attitude is common to both sides of the tracks. It is that way all over the Delta, and no wonder. The lives of Deltans are cut from the same cloth, regardless of skin color.

"Black and white people have been working and living together here since they brought my ancestors over as slaves from West Africa," said Ernest White, seventy-nine, a longtime resident of Humphreys County. "We're on our way back to that, and if we just keep pushing we'll get back to where we live and work together. We've got to respect each other. There should be nothing to keep us from working and living together like the Lord desires us to live. Shouldn't be anything.

"Shouldn't be," he said again, and laughed, shaking his head at how far that is from the reality he has grown old with over eight decades in the Delta. His deep brown skin is worn and polished by the years, and his hair is pure white, eyebrows snow-white above lively dark eyes. He has a strong, strong presence, a lean man with big hands and a straight back.

Ernest White was a farmer for most of his life, working both other people's land and his own. He was raised in a family of fifteen on a

farm in Yazoo County. When he was in the ninth grade he quit school to go to work full-time. His whole family lived on about $400 a year and whatever they could put by. As a young man, he married and moved to Humphreys County to work fifty acres of his own, but during the Depression he had to work for others for fifty cents a day: "Cash money, and I was glad to get it. Working from 'can to can't'— just barely can see to can't see—sun-up to sun-down.

"My wife and I made it on eight dollars a month. Of course, you could buy a steak in those days for ten cents. We made it. I fished and we raised all our vegetables. We banked up sweet potatoes for the winter. Piled them up, got some corn stalks to put over them and put a little hay on top of the corn stalks. Cover that with dirt and they'd keep all winter. By spring, what you hadn't eaten would be dried out, and you took those and used them for slips. You didn't need to go to town each year to buy slips to plant, you raised your own."

He and his wife brought up two sons on their fifty acres, and both children got university degrees. White kept his farm until 1974. Then, with his sons grown and gone, he stopped farming. A widower now, he has more time to give to the other work he has done all his life: as a leader in the black community of Humphreys County. When I met him he was in his second term as a city alderman in Belzoni, and spent each weekday from 1:00 to 5:00 P.M. working in the small offices of the nonprofit community group, the Humphreys County Union for Progress, on the black side of Belzoni's tracks, where he helped out whoever needed it.

The first time I went to see him, I waited on an old, worn, spring-sprung sofa set against a wall, while he sat at a desk and filled out forms for a seventy-four-year-old man. White read the questions and recorded the man's answers. The form requested a little emergency assistance from a federal agency because the man's wife was sick and he had bought medicine, leaving him unable to pay his light bill. The man could neither read nor write, like over a third of the

black adult citizens of Humphreys County, and White went through the questions slowly and patiently with him.

It was just another day trying to help with whatever problems came in the door, another day in a long life of working to put wrongs right, something White had been doing since the mid-1950s, when racial tensions were so fierce in Belzoni that the Reverend George Lee was gunned down on the streets for trying to register voters. "He was a Baptist preacher lived right down the street here, ran a raggedy little old grocery store," said White. "He advocated Negroes going to register to vote, and because of that the whites picked him out as the leader in the community and decided to get rid of him. They killed him, but it didn't do them no good. The more they killed, the stronger we got."

Lee's successor as leader of the local NAACP, Gus Courts, was shot as he stood in his own store by someone in a passing car who gunned him down through the store window. It was White who drove Courts to a black doctor in Indianola, fearing the man would be killed by any Humphreys County doctor. Courts survived and moved away. White stayed right where he was, but was always marked as a man who would not live on his knees. For a long time, that was enough to get a person killed in Belzoni.

"Down here it was tough. You ran a lot of risks fighting for your rights in those times. You never knew what might happen. You could be dead like that," White said, snapping his fingers. "You could meet the citizens' council on any road. They kept track of you—if you went out of town they knew it. We had a sheriff here who was tough on black folks. I don't guess I'll call his name to you, but he was tough. Now he's gone. Passed away."

Things have improved some, he told me, and there are more opportunities for black people in the Delta, but not many more. Ernest White was under no illusions that his white neighbors would ever give him the slightest piece of the pie were it not for federal law. "Things have changed here, but not voluntarily. Nothing changed

voluntarily. The opportunities we have now are because we risked our lives for them, some of us were slain for them, some of us were beat for them, some had their houses burned down, churches were burned, little children died.

"The government had to come in—they knew it was just too bad. We got our vote, thanks to presidents Kennedy and Johnson, and the good Lord. We're poor down here, we don't have a lot of money, but we've got the vote. We might be poor, but we can get elected. I remember the day I couldn't vote, but right now we've got three black county supervisors out of five on the board."

One of those three county supervisors—the second African-American elected to public office in Humphreys County in this century—is Henry Reed, one of only two black catfish farmers in the Delta that I heard about, compared to about four hundred white fish farmers. Three white catfish farmers in the county described Reed in exactly the same way when I asked about him: He farms like a white man, they said. He drives a new pickup and spends most of his time in it. Reed is in his early fifties, tall and broad, with salt-and-pepper mutton-chop sideburns and a trim moustache. "I'm blessed to be in the second year of my second four-year term as a supervisor. My first race was close, but last time I was blessed with seventy-five percent of the vote," he told me, when I talked to him in his Belzoni office.

Reed comes from a long line of Delta farmers, and still works some of the same land that his grandfather farmed. For thirteen years after he graduated from college, he taught school in Indianola during the day and farmed a small piece of land in the early mornings and the late afternoons. In 1979, he decided to get out of teaching and try his hand at full-time farming. He was growing row crops when the catfish business really started to take off in 1984 and 1985.

Reed started talking to people about catfish and eventually be-

came part of a nationwide investment group, which started a minority-owned company called Aquaculture Technology. This company, headquartered in Lafayette, Louisiana, markets catfish under the Le Topper label in North America, Europe, and Africa. Le Topper has 130 ponds north of Lafayette for growing fish and also maintains Reed's nineteen ponds, six of which are brood ponds for providing eggs, and thirteen of which are used for growing fry into fingerlings to stock the ponds in Louisiana.

Spring is when the catfish spawn, and I asked Reed if I could go out with his workers to collect the fertilized eggs from the old ammunition cans that farmers sink in ponds to serve as nests. "You can if you're not scared to stick your hand in there with that male," he said. "It's just like they say about a dog—that fish can smell fear on you, and if you're scared you can get hurt."

In the wild, the male searches out a dark hole beneath brush or up under a bank, cleans it out, and uses his tail to fan a bed—a slight bowl in the mud at the bottom in which eggs can be laid. Then he goes out and finds a female to bring to the nest. The same behavior goes on in the brood ponds, except that the farmer provides plenty of dark holes in the pond by sinking rows of large, five-gallon Army surplus ammo cans, which fill with water and make the perfect place for a male catfish to raise a family. The six-inch hole in the top of the can is just the right size to admit a big brood male. The females lay their eggs, whether in the can or on the river bottom, and leave—as casual a maternity as any known. The male hovers in the water over the eggs, fanning them with his tail to keep them oxygenated. Except for feeding forays, he tends the eggs for seven or eight days until they hatch.

Cans are checked for eggs every two days. Each is attached by a foot-long piece of nylon rope to a piece of cork floating on the surface. Workers "run" the cans by putting on chest waders, getting in the pond, and slogging from float to float, hoisting each can up with one hand far enough to reach in with the other and check for a web of egg mass adhered to the side of the can. The problem is that a

four-pound catfish guarding his eggs can wreak a lot of damage on a human hand in a confined space, and the workers cannot wear gloves to protect against being spiked or bitten because the egg mass must be handled delicately or it will break up into individual eggs, too small to retrieve.

"Some guys can run those cans day in and day out and never have anything happen to them," Reed told me. "Other guys just can't. I've seen some near fatal accidents. Last year we had a guy get bit on the arm by a catfish and it was a tremendous gash. A bite, not a fin. Luckily, that's pretty rare."

Too late, I remembered that you best be careful what you ask for, because you might get it. By the time Reed had finished explaining how eggs were gathered, I began to wish I had kept my mouth shut about giving it a try. His efforts to reassure me offered little in the way of comfort.

"Most of the time it's not difficult if you're not afraid. Each man comes up with his own little technique for getting that male out of there, or getting those eggs while he's still in there without getting attacked. The cans are in pretty shallow water, and most of the time if you raise them up a certain way that fish'll come on out and you can put your hand in. Sometimes he won't, though."

I said, "Uh-huh, uh-huh," about five times, fast, as if all this was the most remarkable thing I had ever heard, while floundering desperately around in my mind for some excuse to regretfully withdraw my request to gather eggs. I couldn't find one. We set a date, a week hence, for me to go out to his hatchery and help collect a morning's worth of spawn.

The appointed day found me at the hatchery, a mile down a dirt road not far beyond the Yazoo River, just northeast of Belzoni. From the outside, the hatchery was little more than a big shed, wood-framed, tin-roofed. The foreman, Fletcher Banks, a solid, square, middle-aged dark-skinned man, was waiting for me in a pickup truck with Marion Reed, his tall, gangling helper. Fletcher did little to soothe my anxiety.

"Aw sure, you can get hurt, but most of the time it's nothing," he said, in response to a question I had tried to ask in a casual tone. "You get finned all the time, but it's not too bad unless you step on a fish and that spike really gets driven up in your foot."

Marion showed me a thick scar down at the base of his right hand by his wrist, where it took five stitches to close a wound from a catfish bite. "He didn't know which way to go when that fish grabbed holt of him," Fletcher laughed. "He was all tore up."

If you keep your palms flat against the side of the can while you feel around for eggs, the male won't be able to spike or bite you, Fletcher told me, but if you stick your hand in there and wave it around, look out. While a four-pound catfish defending his territory by clenching his jaws and sandpaper teeth on the end of your hand may not be as bad as getting chomped by an alligator, or a shark, or a piranha, it looked like a lot more than a painful nip. Fletcher found an extra pair of chest waders for me and off we went.

We had three ponds to run, four hundred cans in all. It was a sunny Saturday morning, and I had the window seat in the pickup. We jounced and rattled over dirt roads between fields where the first upreaching green of soybean plants covered the dark earth. I draped my arm out the truck window and felt the warm sun on it. As we drove up to the pond, a great blue heron rose up off the levee, its wide wings lifting it into the air.

I followed Fletcher and Marion into the pond. The water came up to my belly. "Grab hold," Fletcher told me, pointing to a line of fist-sized corks bobbing a foot out from the bank. "These corks don't have anybody's name on them."

I watched Fletcher work a can and tried to imitate him. I waded through the pond, soft beneath my waders. I went to a cork and hauled on the nylon rope beneath it, raising the can off the bottom and hoisting it up to where I could prop a corner of it on the thigh of my waders with my left hand. Then I tipped the water slowly out, while I eased my right hand into that dark hole at the top of the can.

"No, no," Fletcher said, "your hand is turned up. Keep your palm down. You'll feel the eggs if they're in there.

"Here, there's a bunch in this one, come get them," he called me to his side, a can propped up on his thigh. "Reach in there and get those."

I did, and felt the rubbery egg mass. I slid my hand beneath it and peeled it away from the side of the can, then slowly eased my hand back out the hole at the top. The eggs filled up my cupped palms and ran over the sides of my hands, lemon-yellow eggs in a darker yellow web. Marion pulled along a floating inner tube with an ice chest perched on top of it. This is where the eggs were kept for the trip back to the hatchery, and I slogged back to it and deposited my handful.

By the time we had finished running the four hundred cans, I had learned the moves. If you reached in and touched the bulk of a fish, you pulled your hand out, reached down for the can's bottom, and hauled it up, tilting it so the water inside ran out the top. After a bit, the fish would exit, its flat head momentarily wedged in the can's hole, flapping angrily as it spilled out into the pond in a rush and splash of water. In the cans where there were eggs, there was almost always a fish. From those four hundred cans we gathered over one hundred thousand catfish eggs, which we brought back to the hatchery in the ice chest.

All hatcheries look pretty much alike, differing only in scale—from Henry Reed's four million eggs a year to Jimmy Grant's forty million, a few miles up the road in Isola. A hatchery, regardless of its numbers, consists of rows of long tables with foot-deep stainless steel troughs set into them and filled with water. Mesh baskets, about the size and shape of those used to deep-fry French fries in restaurants, are suspended underwater in the troughs every couple of feet. A pipe runs just above them for the length of the table, and

from it hang slightly curved steel paddles about three inches wide and a foot long. An electric motor turns the pipe and the metal paddles go around and around, cutting a swath through the water beside the baskets, agitating and aerating the water in a mechanical imitation of the fanning action of a male catfish's tail. The pipes turn constantly and dip the paddles into the water every few seconds. The gentle splashing they make, a low suspiration, and the hum of the motors are the dominant sounds in any hatchery.

The eggs are brought into the hatchery from the brood ponds and put in the baskets, one egg mass per basket. Over the course of five or six days the eggs turn color, from lemon yellow to dark brown. By then, the naked eye can see the tiny fry moving inside the egg, and there are two little black dots of eyes in each one. If you pick up an egg mass at this point, it is vibrating, pulsating with the energy of imminent birth, and you can feel each egg quiver and blip against your fingers. In another day, the fry will hatch and separate from the gelatinous mass, falling through the mesh of the basket and into the trough below. The newly-hatched fry look like tadpoles or spermatazoa, made up mostly of a lashing tail and a tiny body, but after a couple of days at the bottom of the trough, each will have two little whiskers, a thin filament at each corner of its mouth. For the first couple of days, the fry will feed off the egg sac that still clings to them. When that is consumed, they will begin coming to the surface to eat the dust-fine feed scattered there. In another two days they will be dipped out of the troughs with an aquarium net and live-hauled to a pond where they will grow into fingerlings to be sold to farmers who raise food fish. When they are first moved from the hatchery to a pond, the fry are still so small that thousands of them would fit in a styrofoam coffee cup.

Catfish like to school together, whether in a pond or a hatchery. Perhaps that is because they were attached to each other even before birth in that rubbery mass of eggs. For whatever reason, schooling behavior is apparent from the moment they hit the bottom of the trough. They congregate there like lead filings on a magnet, gath-

ered together in a ragged ball that constantly changes shape as the fry come and go, shifting positions. Hatchery workers say fry are ready to go into a pond when you put your hand down into the mass of them and they scatter. This indicates that if they are schooled-up close to a pond bank and a frog jumps in the water, they will be able to escape. Sonar imaging has revealed that the adults aggregate in large clumps around a pond, and stay with that same group, in the same part of the pond, for most of their lives.

Jimmy Grant is not one of those guys who farms from a pickup. Six months a year—from the beginning of spawning season in May until the farmers quit buying fingerlings for their ponds in October—he puts in long, eighteen-hour days.

"Yeah, sure, I work like crazy for six months, but I net $400,000 a year," he said. "And the other six months it's pretty easy. From November on, I'm just working in the daytime, all I do is run around and chase birds off ponds. I don't turn the hatchery on until the first of May, but when I turn it on I know it's going to be eighteen hour days until the fifteenth of October.

"There's more money in it than you might think, but there's also lots of stress. I think catfish farming has a lot to do with me being single, all that stress. My two ex-wives are living all right from catfish, though." He laughed ruefully and twisted the heavy gold signet ring, embossed with a catfish, that he wears on his wedding finger. He is in his mid-forties, stout, with a trimmed dark moustache and circles under tired eyes.

"There's a hundred thousand dollars worth of eggs and eyeballs in this hatchery, and they're only good for twenty minutes if the electricity goes off—that right there'll keep you up eighteen hours a day. Just last week a truck driver backed up and tore a whole electric pole out and we had to run the generator for about three hours."

He does his own oxygen checking in the brood ponds. "Every

pond I've got is worth thirty thousand dollars, and I've got twenty-seven ponds. In a crisis situation like you get here in the summer when we're in oxygen-stressed weather, your oxygen checker may decide to go out and drink a pint of Crown that night and he's tired. He makes his 11 P.M. check and figures he'll take a little nap. Now, what if he wakes up at 5 A.M.? You're liable to have lost five or six ponds. I'd rather check them myself. How much can you pay a man to do a good job of guarding your livelihood? I can't feel comfortable doing that."

Not many farmers do feel wholly comfortable about it, whether they raise fingerlings like Jimmy Grant, or have their ponds full of food fish on the way to one and a half pounds and the processing plant. Nevertheless, plenty of them do leave their ponds in other hands at night.

The work of checking oxygen in a pond is simple and monotonous, but absolutely critical. All it requires is visiting each pond once every two hours and writing down the oxygen level therein, obtained by standing on the bank and wagging a bulbous probe, taped to the end of a long, flexible metal pole, back and forth in the water. A cord runs from the bulb, up the pole, to an oxygen meter that the checker holds with the hand not wagging the stick. If the oxygen level falls below four parts per million (ppm), the fish will begin to experience difficulty breathing and will come to the surface looking for oxygen. Below two ppm, they will suffocate, and an entire pond can be wiped out in half an hour.

From May through October, the oxygen level in most ponds is likely to fall below the critical four ppm level on occasional nights. In some of them it will happen once or twice a season, in others once or twice a week. Whenever it happens, it constitutes an emergency and must be dealt with immediately by aerating the pond.

Aeration is done in one of two ways: a set of paddlewheels, or a floating aerator, which is basically an electric pump mounted on a floating platform that throws water into the air. This is far cleaner and more economical than running paddlewheels off tractors, but

the floating aerator cannot be moved around the pond. It needs to be stationary so it can be connected to a light pole on the bank. Fish learn quickly to come to either paddlewheels or aerators if oxygen is low, but most farmers want the capability of aerating different parts of the pond, so they usually keep both tractors and a floating aerator ready to put into action in an oxygen crisis. Many catfish farmers have lost a pond to lack of oxygen at some point in their careers, but the good ones do not let it happen twice. When they speak about it, their voices retain the shock they felt at first seeing a pond full of dead fish.

"It's an awful sight," said Billy Ed Tinnan, a tall, broad man in his sixties, with a shock of white hair over a flushed face, who farms catfish, and owns Tinnan Oil Company, a gas station and garage on Highway 49 in Inverness, about eight miles south of Indianola. "I remember one night I'd checked the oxygen at 2:30 A.M. and saw it was going down, but I didn't think it was too bad, nothing to worry about. I went back at 4:30. I pulled my truck up on the levee, and there wasn't a thing in the headlights but white bellies floating on that pond. That's how fast it can happen."

It is not easy to wake up in the early morning every two hours, stumble out into the humid night, and go check oxygen levels. It is hard farming, far removed from working a row-crop farm in the air-conditioned cab of a tractor or combine, but the oxygen has to be checked.

"It gets pretty bad out there," Tinnan said. "The mosquitos are so thick on top of the levees that you can rub your hand down your arm and just leave a trail of blood. They aren't the worst, though. The bugs I hate are the midges, or whatever you call them little things. They don't bite, but they get in your nose and throat. Man, when you swallow one of those, you've got to have something to drink to get that thing unstuck from your throat. When I checked oxygen, I carried warm Coke in the truck with me. It didn't matter what it was so long as it was wet, but I'd have gone crazy without it."

He eventually got tired of checking oxygen levels every night, so he hired a company to do it for him, but he regularly stays awake anyhow and drives out to his ponds. He hides his pickup behind a bush or tree close to a pond with the truck's headlights out, and waits to see if the oxygen checker is coming around on schedule. Sometimes he keeps his foot on the brake pedal so the brake lights shine red out there in the night, and the oxygen checker sees them and knows there is someone checking on *him*.

Oxygen checkers make more than minimum wage, but not a lot more. The job requires someone with enough sense of responsibility to faithfully perform the simple tasks and write down the oxygen levels for each pond at each check, but it does not attract, generally, the sort of worker who can automatically be counted on to have that sense. It is late-night work, there is rarely anyone who checks on the checker, and it is all too easy to write down an estimated oxygen reading without actually checking a pond for the third time during a night.

The company Tinnan hired to do his checking is Fish Management, Inc., headquartered in Inverness, which manages over one hundred catfish ponds for seven area farmers. Charles Kirksey, twenty-three, is one of Fish Management's oxygen checkers. When I met him, it was his second season. He was diligent about his job, and the company had recognized it by keeping him on the payroll after October and having him do odd jobs over the winter until oxygen-checking season rolled around again the following May. He is blond, lithe, and muscular, and wore a T-shirt and jeans the night I joined him on his rounds. Mud was splattered and dried all over the company pickup that was his to drive day and night. "You can tell an oxygen man by the truck he drives: dirty," he laughed.

The truck was a 1989, full-sized Dodge, which cost the company $13,000. Kirksey said he put almost ten thousand miles a month on it, just checking ponds. From 9:30 P.M. until 7:30 A.M. he had to check seventy-two ponds, three times each, taking oxygen readings and writing them down on the clipboard that rested on the truck's

seat between us. Also between us was the pole with the oxygen probe taped on it and a .22 rifle, barrel down on the pickup floor, stock resting beside my leg on the seat.

Kirksey had a spotlight plugged into the truck's cigarette lighter. He held the light out the window with his left hand, playing it across the ponds as we drove slowly by on the levee, while he steered with his right hand. He kept a sharp eye out for any sign of fish at the surface, which is the first and only way that fish indicate low oxygen in their ponds. At one point, he stopped the truck as we drew even with an aerator floating in a pond near the bank. Wrapped around one corner of its platform frame, stark and menacing in the light's beam, was a thick water moccasin. Kirksey brought the .22 up from the seat with his right hand, laid it out the window resting on the door frame, and squeezed off a shot. The snake fell into the water with a splash.

When he stopped the truck to check a pond, he left the motor running in neutral, with the door open. That way he could take his reading, get right back in the truck and write it down by the overhead light that only worked if the truck's door was open, then shift into drive and be off to the next pond. The levees are so flat he did not need to use his emergency brake when he left the truck. There was no time to waste if he was to get all the readings for all the ponds.

Clouds of midges swirled over the ponds in the beam of the spotlight, and made a beeline for the illuminated cab of the truck where I sat waiting for Kirksey to take his readings. They look like mosquitos, but fortunately midges do not bite. Unfortunately, their insubstantial bodies, thin legs, and gossamer wings easily fit in facial cavities, down the throat, up the nose, or in the ear.

"They're awful when you get one in your eye," he told me. "They get up against your eyeball and they're hard as hell to get out, your eye drives you crazy all night."

In no time, dead midges lay in a patina across the windshield, a long, wide smear, while inside the cab I stopped trying to brush

them away after a while and just suffered them to swarm on and around me. Snakes and bugs are not the only wildlife to be found around ponds late at night. There was an intermittent croaking of bullfrogs, and Kirksey said he had heard wolves howling. He said he had also seen coyotes, foxes, and "beaucoup coons." As we drove down a dirt road beside a field, on the way from one set of ponds to the next, he played the spotlight out the window, across an expanse of green, waist-high wheat ending by a distant line of trees. Out in the field, the light hit something and two eyes sparkled ruby red in the glare, the shadowy shape of a deer barely visible behind them.

"They like to graze in the wheat," he said. "You wouldn't believe how many's in there sometimes."

There was a half-moon over the dark waters, its silvery light rippling in a slight breeze on the surface of the ponds. Kirksey had a country and western station on the truck's radio, coming in from Jackson. Singers like Eddie Rabbit, Mickey Gilley, and Merle Haggard, engineered in high-tech Nashville studios, kept the oxygen checkers company when they were the only human beings awake for miles around, their mournful music booming out across the ponds in the empty moonlit reaches of the Delta.

Kirksey takes home about $300 a week for seventy hours of work, plus he has the use of the truck and a company house to live in with his wife and children, located by one of Fish Management's own catfish ponds. His wife brought two young kids to their marriage and they had another one. Living by a pond, even rent-free, can be a mixed blessing.

"The other day a moccasin got up under the carport. The kids were playing outside and come in saying, 'Snake, snake . . .'

"They woke me up, which I knew meant they were serious, 'cause they generally know to let me sleep during the day. I went out and killed it, but, you know, my fifteen-month-old boy might have crawled up under there with that snake and been bit. He'd have died. I like living out in the country, but that's not the first moccasin I've killed close to the house."

For kids in the Delta, baseball is the sport of choice, with football and basketball running way behind, and soccer further back yet. The black kids have their own league, organized by the city's department of parks and recreation, and some of the teams have local sponsors and rudimentary uniforms, but they do not take kids' baseball to an extreme like the white people across the tracks. They have neither the time, nor the money to invest. The white kids—all boys, girls do not play—join organized teams from the time they are six years old. Each team is sponsored locally, but each has perfect, scaled-down replicas of a major league team's uniform, and they use the big league names. These teams are not affiliated with the Little League, but with something called the Dixie Youth Association. The fields are well kept, with good lights, working scoreboards, and bleachers behind home plate. The games begin each afternoon, shortly after school lets out. Night baseball is out of the question because of the mosquitos. When the lights come on in the early evening for the last game of the day, the mosquitos begin to pester and annoy players and spectators alike, attracted to the thick heat and clumps of people under the lights.

I went down to the baseball park a few times. For me, live baseball at day's end is always a pleasant way to set down the burden of the world for a while and lose myself in the strategies and rhythms of the sport. Spring and summer trigger an urge to watch baseball, and the park at the edge of town seemed like a good place to walk in the late afternoon. It is true that ten-year-olds cannot be expected to perform a flawless rendition of the national pastime, but kids playing, even with all their errors and awkwardness, is okay, if that is all the baseball there is to see.

What bothered me about watching the games in Indianola was not the lack of skill, but those major league uniforms, with names like Mets, Red Sox, and Yankees written on them, worn by all-white teams. Segregated baseball ruined the game for me. Baseball was,

after all, one of the first arenas of American public life in which it was explicitly declared that all Americans could have an opportunity to do equally well. The integration of baseball in 1947, for all the racial inequities that still exist in the game, was a notable step forward, and it was unpleasant to see it reversed, in 1990, in Indianola.

The two leagues from different sides of the tracks never meet, and parents never get to sit in the same bleachers and discover the commonality of cheering for their kids' teams, of slapping at mosquitos, and fending off demands from siblings of the players for Cokes and popcorn. I gave up stopping at the ball park. Instead, I would just keep walking, going on out into the country where neither black nor white people amounted to a hill of beans against the immense, open sky.

Federal civil rights laws have helped assure that "separate-but-equal" will, at least, be pretty much equal—public parks and schools must be available to all, and municipal jobs must be open to both races—but what cannot be legislated is the recognition of a common humanity more basic than legal protection. Black and white Deltans almost never interact with each other in a purely human, social fashion, and rarely see the sameness in how they live their lives: people on both sides of town spend their Saturdays cutting the grass, washing their cars, and cheering for their kids, yet they never do it together. In addition to narrowing every facet of their individual lives, this attitude has had severe economic consequences. Corporations, industries, and individuals steer clear of moving to the Delta because of this de facto apartheid, and the best and brightest kids of both races leave and put their talents to use elsewhere.

"The communities in the Delta are swimming upstream, against the current, because of so many decades of educational neglect, because of all those years of bias and prejudice, which have economically crippled that part of the state," Dick Molpus, the secretary of state, told me when I talked to him in his Jackson office. "In addi-

tion, changing trends in industry and economy have made jobs hard to find, and the demographic trend has also been against the people in the Delta—the population is going down. It's an uphill battle."

Molpus, thirty-eight, is a young, zealous, and apparently honest secretary of state, part of a new breed of forward-looking Mississippi politicians. Urbane and well-spoken, he is a man frequently mentioned as a future gubernatorial candidate. He was born in Philadelphia, Mississippi, and his feelings about race were forged in a youth marked by the murders of Goodman, Cheney, and Schwerner in his hometown.

"What I hope is going to happen in the next decade is that some communities in the Delta recognize that to be 'winner' communities they are going to have to lift the entire community up, both black and white, stop the divisiveness, and recognize, for example, that public schools have to be a magnet to attract new industry and new jobs," Molpus told me. "There are businesses that will come to the Delta if the quality of life there is attractive enough. That's got to be what happens, or we're facing some incredibly dismal trends there. I think the jury's still out on which one it will be. We'll see."

Lonesome, 'round midnight, I sat contemplating these and other matters, sipping a glass of bourbon and ice on the screened-in verandah of my rented home. Western Avenue, which runs in front of the house, is divided by the railroad tracks. The house looks across a broad front yard to the tracks, and the backyard slopes down to Indian Bayou. Two trains go by each night, one at 10:30 P.M. and one at 2 A.M., but after a couple of weeks I had stopped waking up as the late one clanked, jangled, and rumbled by outside. I was, however, usually awake when the early one rolled through, and this night I toasted it from the verandah, where I whiled away the hours in the warm night air. It was not hard to lose track of time, sitting there and contemplating my life from the perspective and distance

of the Delta. The occasional car or truck passed on Western Avenue, and I heard the piercing single-note call of some night bird.

I could see half a nighttime sky's worth of stars—the heavens were usually clear and crowded over the Delta. A full moon broke free from the silhouetted branches of the huge pecan tree in the front yard and rose into sight through the noisy night. There was an intermittent crackling from the blue-light bug killer beside the house next door, katydids in the pecan tree buzzed in rising and falling tides of sound, and the frogs cheeped and peeped in Indian Bayou, down behind the house.

CHAPTER VI

Educating the Delta

FOR THE first half of the twentieth century, business-as-usual in the Delta required a steady supply of cheap and available labor. Black people were held in an economic bondage, kept in debt and out of school, scuffling desperately just to stay alive and feed their families. Then, as now, there was a poverty deeper than most anywhere else in our country, as if the remoteness and foreignness of the Delta kept many of its citizens from having access to things that most of us take for granted as a birthright of being born North Americans—things like running water, a visit to the doctor, enough to eat.

"My ancestors came and cleared out the swamps for the 'marster,' and then they sharecropped it," Ernest White told me one afternoon

in the offices of the Humphreys County Union for Progress, in-between visits from people who needed his assistance. "I remember clearing land myself, many a time. You'd go up to work in what we called 'the deadening.' You'd deaden the trees, and after a while the limbs would start dropping off and you'd go back and pile them up, then eventually the tree would fall and you'd set everything on fire.

"They'd have a big bell mounted up on wood, and that bell would ring around four-thirty in the morning for you to go to the fields. You'd get up and it'd still be dark, and you'd eat your breakfast by lamplight, maybe have some fatback, or some cornbread with sorghum.

"The hosteler, the man at the lot, he'd have the mules fed and ready to go to work when you got there. You know, we used mules to haul the trees out to where they could be burned. At noon, that bell would ring again. We had mules that would stop working as soon as they heard that noon bell. They knew what it meant. Then, an hour later, you'd go back out and work until sundown. I did all that for fifty cents a day."

When Ernest White was young, few black men stayed in school long enough to reach a high school level. Most black kids went to school during the six months when there was nothing that needed doing in the cotton fields, and when they reached the age of thirteen they generally stopped going altogether. Even those whose thirst for learning kept them in school were only able to go through the eleventh grade in Indianola or Belzoni. Past that, they had to be sent off to board at a black college, not an easy thing for a poor family to finance.

"For men who didn't want to farm, there was nothing to do but preach or teach," White told me. "You couldn't do things like work in a bank or be a police officer. That's why so many men with dark skins went into teaching in the black schools. Now, that has changed. Kids today can go to school, ride the bus there and back, spend the day there, and get something to eat. Those who really want to can make something of themselves, today."

Education always seemed to black Deltans like the best way out of poverty. More than fifty years ago, Powdermaker wrote in *After Freedom:*

> The faith of the present-day Negroes in education is much like the faith of those Americans who set up the public school system. They looked to education as the great and indispensable foundation of democracy. Education was to fit every citizen for participation in government, and to spread the doctrine that every citizen should be allowed to participate. It was viewed as the gateway to equal opportunity, the threshold of a new and better life.

The struggle for education and voting rights was the flashpoint for a second civil war between Mississippi and the federal government, which began in the Delta almost a century after the first one ended. It started in 1954 with the ruling by the Supreme Court that mandated integrated public schools. That second war was still going on when I got to the Delta. The mistake of taking up arms against the union and sacrificing so many young lives to a lost cause was not repeated. Instead, the tactic was evasion rather than direct resistance.

Over the decade after the public schools were integrated, private academies, offering grades one through twelve and catering exclusively to white children, sprang up like mushrooms around the Delta. Black kids went to the public schools and found themselves alone there. Indianola Academy was founded in 1964, and, until recently, all white Indianolan youngsters, except those from the poorest families, have gone there. Any white parents who thought in terms of college and career for their child would scrape up the money for tuition at Indianola Academy. It is not cheap, running around $2,000 per year in 1990, with a break of a few hundred dollars for subsequent kids from the same family who attend the academy at the same time.

I met one white Indianolan who had not been able to afford to send his children to the academy, and there had been no help offered by the school. This was during the late 1960s, when the academy

cost $500 a year. He had paid for his son to finish school there, barely able to get the tuition money together, but he could not afford to send his two daughters.

"That July, they sent me a form asking for $250 apiece to reserve a space for them, and they wanted me to sign the enclosed contract for the other $250," he told me. "I ran into the academy's lawyer downtown at the drugstore fountain one evening. He asked me was I going to register my girls and had I got the form? I told him it was on top of the icebox where I'd tossed it. Then he asked if I didn't aim to get my girls an education? I said yes, but I couldn't afford to do it at the academy.

"One thing led to another and he called me a nigger lover, right there in the drugstore. I picked up a chair and that's as far as it went. I ain't heard nary a thing from the academy since, nor they from me. I'm no nigger lover, although I've lived close to colored folks all my life. I generally go by what a fellow does. My kids did all right in public school."

The academy is tax exempt as a nonprofit corporation, but in order to keep that status it is required to have a nondiscriminatory admissions policy. In fact, during the years since 1964, only one black student—a girl—was admitted, but she did not last there, lonely and solitary, more than a couple of years. In over twenty-five years, there has just been that one little girl, and not a single black faculty member has ever taught there. The white community turned the public schools over to black students, and supported public education at the minimum level to keep the schools open. For most of those years, the public school system's administrative and management-level jobs went to white people, who sent their own children to the academy.

Most white parents complain and grumble about having to send their children to the academy. Nobody likes paying the academy's steep tuition for twelve years per child at the same time they have to pay taxes to the Indianola Public School District to keep public schools up and running. Nevertheless, even the most liberal of white

Indianolans send their children to the academy, claiming that is the only way to get them an education that will prepare them for college. The academy's entire curriculum is geared to standardized tests, and students in the academy's high school test well on college admissions exams like the ACT and the SAT—far better than their peers at the public Gentry High School. Teachers at Gentry concede this point, but add that the focus at their school is not so much on preparation for higher education, as on preparation for functioning and reasoning out in the world. Public school teachers describe the Indianola Academy students as programmed, and claim they spend most of their time learning by rote.

The irony is that when the white students from the Delta's private academies reach a college or university, they are in classes with plenty of black students and an occasional black professor. This is true whether they go off to Ole Miss or Harvard, or stay at home and attend Delta Community College in nearby Moorhead or Delta State University in Cleveland. Because of the federal funds available in grants and loans, poor blacks and whites who want to do so can often afford to go to college, and there are plenty who do. The extraordinary amount of money spent on keeping the Delta's races apart through the twelfth grade actually sends the white students to college with a handicap, because they find themselves competing with members of other races and being taught by them. Those of both the black and white races who do not go to college after high school frequently join a branch of the military, and there the white kids are at a particular disadvantage, because they are totally unprepared for working cooperatively with black people, living with them, and even taking orders from them.

"To me, the academy situation came about because of what I call the older heads. It was the older generation that brought the academies about," said Henry Reed, the black Humphreys County supervisor and catfish farmer who spent thirteen years teaching at Gentry High School in Indianola.

"The younger generation now, when they leave the academies

and go to college, they mix, and they accept each other. Maybe not all of them, but the bulk of them accept each other. My son is in a private Catholic school in Greenville and they accept each other, no problem.

"If the old heads had not put the academies there, the younger generation wouldn't keep them. There are white guys younger than I am who have kids at the academy, but they want them to come to public school. Their kids go through the twelfth grade affiliating only with whites, but when they leave the academy, those kids are going to have to mix if they're going to stay on this earth. Still, the young ones feel the pressure from the old heads, and the social thing makes them keep their kids in the academy, even though they don't want to and it costs so much."

Catfish money pays for a lot of segregated education in Indianola, and catfish farmers influence a lot of policy at Indianola Academy. In fact, a number of the academy's board are people who earn their livings in the catfish industry. In 1988, when Indianola Academy became the first private school in the country to require that students submit to random drug testing, two of the academy's board members who were vocal in their support for collecting urine specimens from all students above the third grade were Lester Myers and Turner Arant. Both men are big players in the catfish industry.

Turner Arant was chairman of the board of farmer/shareholders at the Delta Pride processing plant when I met him, and had been one of the first farmers to begin raising catfish on a large scale. He was also, along with Tommy Taylor, one of the first people to talk about catfish farming to the media. Arant is often the representative catfish farmer interviewed by journalists. He started raising catfish in 1962, in a pond designed for his family to fish in, and he harvested his first pond commercially in 1965. He kept right at it, and was among the original founders of Delta Pride. In 1986 he was elected chair of Delta Pride's board of directors.

Lester Myers runs Delta Western, the largest producer of catfish feed in the world, whose plant and offices are on Highway 82, at the

western end of Indianola. The mill, with its granaries and smoke stacks, looms up off the flat vista and can be seen from far away in either direction on the highway. The sharp smell of thousands of pounds of roasting grain fills the air around the mill, and, depending on how the wind is blowing, driving past Delta Western on the highway can be quite an olfactory assault.

"The quality of the public education system has really, really eroded away," Myers told me when I interviewed him in his office at the plant. "The whole public education system eroded away."

Wasn't that because the entire white school-age population was pulled out all at once and sent to the academy?

"That too," said Myers, a large, healthy man, who radiates assurance and self-satisfaction. "But, the public school system just eroded away. The quality of education coming out of the academy—if you look at the ACT scores—is far greater than out of the public school system. Public schools have got to upgrade their teachers and deal with the drug problem. At the academy, there wasn't a problem, we were just trying to avoid a problem."

Myers lives on land that fronts Highway 49, about twelve miles south of Indianola down by the Sunflower/Humphreys line. It is the same land on which he was raised. His father row-cropped it. Delta Western, which Myers has administered since its organization in 1979, is a nonprofit farmers cooperative, like Delta Pride, and is tremendously successful. In 1990, the company sold about two hundred thousand tons of feed, worth some $50 million, a percentage of which was rebated to the farmer/owners who bought the feed during the year.

When the first catfish farming began back in the mid-1960s, feed was not only costly, but its supply was uncertain. Ralston-Purina and a number of other companies were making a generic fish feed, and farmers would buy it by the boxcar load. Feed is the catfish

farmer's greatest expense and accounts for about 50 percent of annual operating costs. In those early days, Ralston-Purina was merciless, according to farmers with long memories. They would jack the price of feed up, and what could a farmer do except pay it? When Producer's Feed, the first cooperative feed mill, was formed in 1974 outside of Belzoni, that changed. As the number of farmers with acres under water continued to increase, the need for a second feed mill became clear and Delta Western was formed. Both feed mills are gold mines. One farmer told me that when Delta Western was formed, he paid $20,000 for his stock, which has since increased in value to $450,000.

In addition to serving as executive vice president of Delta Western, Myers has five hundred acres under water, where he grows feed fish, and a half dozen of his twenty-five ponds are between his front porch and Highway 49. Sizeable stretches of the highway between Indianola and Belzoni are lined with ponds, and Myers' are among the nicest to look at. There are ducks and Canadian geese around them, the levees are well tended, and the grass is kept down. At one spot beside the gravel road that leads from the highway to his brick home is a shotgun cabin, a typical Delta sharecropper's shack covered with tar paper, with a wooden porch and a tin roof. Myers had found it somewhere else and brought it back to put on his land as a guest house.

An associate of Myers once took me to see the guest house, turning off Highway 49 just to drive me by it. "Isn't it cute?" he asked. "Lester's got that guest house just like it used to be, a living room, bedroom, kitchen, bathroom, right in a row. To go from the living room to the bathroom you have to pass through the bedroom," he laughed, apparently unaware that a large segment of the Delta's population was still living in houses exactly like it.

Myers styles himself a hunter/conservationist, as do many men in the Delta, where kids are out hunting deer by age ten. Myers' avocation is waterfowl, and he exhibits a truly conservationist attitude toward them. He is the person primarily responsible for the flocks

of Canadian geese that live on many of the catfish ponds. Catfish farmers do not hunt the geese and do not mind if they eat enough fish feed to stay fat and healthy, which they do. While most farmers admit to killing a cormorant or two over the years, usually out of sheer frustration, the idea of killing a goose is genuinely taboo. The Canadian geese have adapted very well to the ponds, building their nests at the edge of levees and laying a clutch of two or three eggs in them. There is always a delighted laugh to be enjoyed at the sight of a pair of Canadians waddling down the levee, herding little goslings in front of them, stretching their necks out and honking menacingly at pickups as they drive by.

The Indianola Academy board was only one of a number Lester Myers has served on, including that of the Delta Council, the most influential body of power-brokers in the state. He is also at home in the world of high finance and global markets. The price of catfish feed can change daily, depending on what happens to the price of grain during the course of a business day on the Board of Trade exchange in Chicago, which in turn can depend on the course of world events in places as far away as the Soviet Union or Saudi Arabia.

From his office at Delta Western, Myers keeps a careful weather eye on the Board of Trade. At one end of his broad desk is a television, hooked up to a satellite dish outside the plant. The screen lists grain prices throughout the day. The grains of interest to an executive of a catfish feed mill are soybeans, wheat, and corn. Catfish feed is a mix of 50 percent soybean meal, 8 to 12 percent fish meal, a little wheat to bind it, a little vitamin-mineral mix for good health, and corn to make the whole thing float. It is formulated to provide the fish with food that is 32 percent protein.

Myers frequently finds himself in a position to address policy issues, whether for Indianola Academy or the Delta Council. He leaned back in the chair behind his desk to talk to me, one small part of his attention always on the prices being shown on the television screen, and considered the Delta's pervasive poverty.

"I was out at Delta Pride last week—they employ about eighteen

hundred people—and they told me they had a ten percent turnover most months. Those people don't really want to work. The government programs pay so high that some of these people just don't want to work. And it's hard to upgrade the economy if you have some people who just don't have the desire to work when they can sit back and draw government programs. We have over eighty-five people working here and our biggest problem is finding good workers."

It is no secret that the Delta is losing population at a noticeable rate. Myers estimated, sadly, that only one in six Deltans who graduated from college would come back home to live. If those other five graduates were not from wealthy families, already growing catfish or cotton or running a feed mill, or already embedded in the economy with a leg up on good fortune, it was going to be hard for them to find a way to make a decent living, particularly if they were black.

Catfish farmers unanimously told me that their major expense was feed and their major headache was labor turnover. They cannot get, nor keep, good help. Even if they only have a couple of hundred acres in ponds, and need only five or six men (willing to work for low wages and no benefits) to mow, drive tractors, walk through the pond behind a seine net, and gather eggs, it is hard to find them and harder to keep them, despite the Delta's high unemployment rate.

"The labor situation here is not good, the labor force is not what we need," said Spooky Bearden, who farms two thousand acres of cotton and an immense spread of 102 ponds with his two brothers. "Our turnover rate on the people making an hourly wage, and even on the people making a weekly salary, is very high, much higher than we would like it."

The Beardens' catfish farm outside Isola is one of the largest in the world, with more than 3,500 acres under water and fifty-five full-time employees to run the operation. They work a seining crew two hundred days a year, and the hatchery, from which they stock their

ponds, produced over one hundred million fry in 1990. The family is headed up by Dillard Bearden, who by 1990 had grown too old to have much to do with running the company. His three sons have each taken some part in running the farm: the oldest, about fifty, short and squat, is called "Spooky" by one and all; the youngest, Bob, in his early forties, had a full beard and a wild look in his eye, and when I saw him, sported a shirt unbuttoned at the top, three gold chains nestled in the hair on his chest, jeans, and cowboy boots; the middle son, Richard, who handles the cotton part of the Beardens' enterprises, was dressed neatly in sports shirt and slacks. He was the only one who could have walked down the street anywhere and not drawn looks. The family has a reputation for fast living and sticking together. It is well known in Humphreys and Sunflower counties that to mess with one Bearden is to mess with all of them.

One of Sunflower County's more respectable citizens wrinkled her nose when I mentioned the Beardens. "That Bob Bearden's just an outlaw," she told me. "Once, years ago, he was driving wild and a policeman tried to pull him over, but Bob wouldn't stop. The policeman chased him home, and when he got there Bob and his father were standing in the yard with rifles. The policeman got out with his gun drawn, but nobody fired—they had a Mexican standoff and finally the policeman left. That's how the Beardens do things."

When I introduced myself to Bob Bearden and told him I was writing a book about the Delta, he told me to write about how the black people cheat the government's welfare programs. "There are a lot of colored who just don't want to work," he said. "Now, they're not all that way. We got a boy raised here on the farm, and he's just a nice boy. He's colored. We probably pay him $20,000 a year. I'd like for a man to see the kind of house he lives in, an old house he owns and pays for each month with the money he's earned and doesn't take a nickel from the government, and then go over there and see the kind of a house those sons-of-guns are living in who won't work, won't teach their kids to work, teach 'em no respect. They've got brand new houses paid for by the government, and they

tear those houses up in no time, and you think they'll work? They don't hit a damned lick at a snake and won't hit one, and have a house payment of about $30 a month."

Dillard Bearden's father, Bob's grandfather, came to Isola in 1925 and bought two hundred acres, which he cleared with hired help, using axes, cross-cut saws, and mules. When Dillard got out of the Army in 1945, his share of the property amounted to only forty acres. While Spooky and his brothers were growing up, their father worked hard and steadily, making a living and gradually acquiring more land. By the time Spooky went to Mississippi State University, did a stint in the Air Force, then came back home, the family's fortunes were on the rise, and eventually they accumulated more than five thousand acres of land.

Today, the Bearden brothers and their father keep an office in Isola's one-block downtown. From this simple headquarters they run a mammoth family enterprise. Tommy Taylor told me, "The Beardens have such a big operation, if they cough twice they're behind." Yet, Spooky finds the time to make regular trips to Las Vegas, and Bob often takes the company plane to Houston or New Orleans where he can do a little business and have a little fun at the same time. Business and pleasure amount to about the same thing for the Bearden brothers. Working-class guys made good through the auspices of catfish farming, they make no pretense of coming from a long line of cotton barons and feel no urge to put on airs. For instance, they can certainly afford to buy their clothes in New York, or Dallas, or anywhere they want, but they buy them from Mohamed's Department Store in Belzoni, run by their friend Ollie Mohamed.

By stringing together good years and expansion loans, the Beardens have created one of the biggest operations in the Delta. However, they have gone about as far as they can go. Too far, said Spooky, with a tinge of sadness in his voice. "We bought this land and put it together as a team, but we don't have a big family coming on. My two brothers each have a son, it's not like we each have three

boys coming on. We've expanded too much and we're too leveraged. One big problem with the catfish pond versus the cotton farm is that if you're growing cotton and decide you want to retire, there's somebody you can rent your farm to or somebody who'll buy it. There's a market for it.

"A catfish farm is not that way. You're pretty much married to a catfish farm. The difference as far as a renter is that the guy who wants to rent your cotton farm won't have to have a lot of money to get additional financing just to grow a crop. If it costs $300 an acre in operating money to produce an acre of cotton and he had $100 an acre in cash, he'd be able to get a loan from the bank for the other $200, and give them a mortgage on the crop. But if you rent an empty pond to a guy, he's got to come up with at least $2,500 an acre in cash money from somewhere to stock the pond, feed it out, and take care of all the production costs before he ever harvests one dollar. The banker can't see his collateral, he can't see those fish growing like he can that cotton."

The Beardens would like to find a buyer for their catfish farm, but people with the kind of money that would be required to operate it are scarce, and those who have that kind of money and want to invest it in catfish are even scarcer. In 1989, they almost struck a deal with an out-of-state consortium of investors. The deal was in negotiation for months, but never materialized.

Other catfish farmers have been luckier in their dealings with outside investors. Turner Arant, for instance, has done very well. After he built his first pond in 1962 for his family to fish in, three years passed before he sold a single fish. "In 1965, I decided to market those fish because there were a bunch of them in there and they were getting big. I called this little processing plant over in McGee, Arkansas, and they sent a harvesting crew and a live-haul truck over here, seined the ponds, loaded the fish, and hauled them ninety

miles back to McGee. A couple of weeks later they sent me a check for a little over $3,000. In 1965, that was like $30,000 today. So I got interested in the business commercially and immediately built a few more ponds."

Arant is an older man with a broad face, dressed in a sports shirt and slacks. His office is a low building by his ponds in northern Sunflower County. "About 1973 or 1974 the cotton situation got really bad," he told me when I talked to him there. "It was getting impossible to make money off of cotton, and every year I'd look at my cash flow on cotton and see that it was the rest of my farm that was carrying it, so I said, 'Heck, I need to just quit growing cotton.' So I did, I quit growing cotton and that freed up a lot of equipment and time, so I started building more ponds. In 1977, it was so tough trying to market the fish that about six of us started talking about how to process them, and in about two years we had about forty farmers together and got a cooperative loan, and started Delta Pride."

In 1990, Arant had 1,600 acres of ponds, owned plenty of shares in both Delta Pride and Delta Western, and also managed 400 acres of ponds for a limited partnership involving investors from all over the country and administered by an investment firm in Memphis. "What I did was buy the land, which I'm selling to the limited partnership, and I'm ending up as the managing partner."

In addition to making a profit on the sale of the land, Arant received $75,000 for seventy-five shares of his Delta Pride stock, which he sold to the limited partnership so it could process the fish it grew. He is also paid a salary as the managing partner.

Turner Arant is a fundamentalist Christian, a strong believer. When I met him, his son had just bought a radio station in Indianola and instituted an all-Christian format. Both of his children had attended the academy, and Arant was on the board. When the media found out about the drug-testing proposal at the academy and national newspaper and television pieces were done about it, Arant stood firm in his public support of the program, although the idea

was opposed editorially by the *Enterprise-Tocsin*, Indianola's weekly newspaper.

There has been a weekly newspaper in the town of Indianola for over a century, and Jim Abbott has been its editor since 1972. Both of Abbott's children went to the academy for all twelve grades. Nevertheless, he took an editorial stand against the school's drug-testing policy and ran an interview with a sixteen-year-old girl, who described how embarrassed she had been when she could not urinate into the bottle provided her, and how the teacher administering the tests had made her drink Cokes until she was able to squeeze out the required few drops. The Indianola Academy's board had voted in favor of the drug tests in 1988, making them mandatory for all students above the third grade. It was still being done in 1990. There had not been a single positive test.

There is no disputing that Indianola, and the whole Delta, has a serious drug problem. This has become much more threatening with the advent of crack cocaine. Crack riddles the Delta, particularly on the black side of the tracks, where unemployment is at its worst and anything that can be sold for fast money is welcomed. Drug-related crimes have increased rapidly with the number of break-ins and armed robberies climbing steadily, year to year. Gangs, supported by crack sales, have sprung up in Greenville, and cocaine arrests are constantly being made throughout the Delta, in small towns with populations of only a couple thousand. Even drive-by gang killings are not uncommon in Greenville, where, it is said, you can have someone killed for $500. Greenville has the second highest per capita crime rate in the South, next to Miami, according to news reports.

There is some good news about public education in Indianola. The number of students at the academy has declined in recent years, while white enrollment in public schools for elementary and middle-

school grades is up. Between 1986 and 1990, enrollment at Indianola Academy, grades one through twelve, fell from 755 students to 492. Many white Deltans have begun enrolling their children in public school until they reach junior high school and puberty.

"Getting ready for college is why they'll tell you they take their kids out of public school in junior high and send them to the academy," one public school teacher, a woman, told me. "But what it really is, is that the parents don't want their white girls going to school with black boys."

It is the old, hoary white man's fear, rooted in the days when slaves and wives were both considered property, one to be protected from the other. The Delta's racism stands on two legs: sex and money. While it's unlikely that either of these will be shaken by the integration of the lower grades, black parents are still relieved to see it happening, because they know whites will be willing to pay for better schools if their own kids are in them. The white parents feel better, too, glad to stop paying such high prices to separate children who are too young even to notice skin color.

The shift toward better public school integration in Indianola directly followed a period of upheaval and confrontation in 1986 between the white and black communities, which was almost as charged as the years of civil rights struggle in the mid-1960s. This time, the issue was who would be superintendent of Indianola's public schools, and, before it was resolved, there was a thirty-five-day black boycott of the town's businesses, which received national media attention.

The old superintendent, who had been on the job for twenty years, resigned under a cloud after the *Enterprise-Tocsin* revealed he was making the third highest salary of any superintendent in the state while steadfastly refusing, year after year, to grant even the smallest of raises to his teachers. The school board, four white members and one black, conducted a search to replace the superintendent following his resignation, initially choosing a white man from out of the county over two qualified black candidates who were school

principals within the Indianola school system. This, in a town where almost no white children had attended a public school for twenty years. White people were controlling the schools' funds and keeping the power for themselves. The black community coalesced behind one of the principals the board had rejected, Robert Merritt, and a boycott was called of both the schools and the downtown stores. Children were kept at home, and no money was spent downtown, except at the Piggly-Wiggly.

Willie Spurlock was one of the black leaders who organized the boycott and served as its spokesman. A stout man in early middle age with salt-and-pepper hair, a moustache, and embouchure beard, he is a lifelong Indianola resident and a father of two. His wife, Patsy Spurlock, is a public school teacher. They live on a quiet street of single-family brick homes.

Willie Spurlock was trained in the crucible of struggle when working as a young man at a freedom school in 1964. A veteran of battles to get what should have been his all along, he is not bitter, militant, or disillusioned. He is hard-working and upright, well-liked by most, and praised for his negotiating skills. When I met him, Spurlock was working as an assistant plant manager in charge of personnel and traffic at the SouthFresh catfish processing plant, just south of Indianola. It is a small plant, processing about five million pounds a year, owned by Julian Allen, a white, fourth-generation Indianolan. Willie Spurlock was the only black person I met in a management job in the catfish industry.

"When the boycott went past two weeks, they saw the handwriting on the wall," he told me. "It was very strong. I don't know if we'll ever stick together like that again, but God gave us His blessing to do it then. We didn't just jump into a boycott. We had written them and met with them and got no response.

"I've been in the retail business myself, and I knew that a man in business, at least here in Indianola, counts on three times of the year to make his money: Christmas, Easter, and back-to-school in the fall. So we hit them right at Easter, and it was very successful. They

made a bad mistake at the beginning. The powers that be said, 'They're not going to do anything. They'll get tired and put those signs down.' There were some merchants that got hurt, but the powers that be came to their rescue by finally doing what was right to begin with."

The school board was forced to buy out the contract of the white man who had first been awarded the job. The money for the buyout was raised privately, primarily from Indianola business people eager to see the boycott come to an end. Robert Merritt was named superintendent. He had remained steadfastly in the background during the boycott, but when the job was offered he was ready. That was in 1986, and since then things have slowly improved. By 1990, the black/white ratio in the public schools had gone from 93 percent black to 85 percent. In November 1988, a $5 million bond issue for public school improvements was passed with 80 percent of the votes.

Merritt has brought his own particular zeal to the office, and he makes it clear that the position of superintendent is more than just another job for him. A solid, compact, light-skinned man, he has a square, dependable face and is carefully, impeccably, and modestly groomed, a man full of dignity and reserve. "I was raised in Aberdeen, Mississippi, and my father had fifteen dollars a month to support us. My daughter is on a full scholarship to Howard University. My son is twenty-six with a degree in computer engineering from Ole Miss, and he works for IBM in Houston," he told me.

"Education is not going to solve all our problems, but it comes closer than anything else I know. Any town will move at about the same rate as its education. Our schools are not what they should be, nor where we want them to be, but we have a road map and we're headed in the right direction. Attitudes are being changed and have been changed. I'm optimistic. We've certainly got our problems, but I'm optimistic."

I interviewed Willie and Patsy Spurlock during a late afternoon in early summer, and it was getting dark when I left their house on its tidy block with neat yards. Martins were hunting mosquitos, swooping through the air beneath the streetlights. I drove on out into the country to watch the sun set. A breeze was blowing, and small, foot-high dust devils were rising up and wheeling across a cotton field like miniature tornados. Even with the breeze, someone was burning a winter wheat field, the flames dancing through the sere fields covered with a white rolling smoke, translucent against the oranges and pinks and golds of day's end.

I came around a curve on the narrow, two-lane road I was traveling, and there was a tumbledown wood cabin set on a small grassy plot in the bend of the road. I got a glimpse of its tilted wooden porch, an old, low sofa on it, and, on the sofa, an ancient black man in a white shirt and a thin, limp sportcoat. His face was as dark as old mahogany, his eyes were set deep under his brow, his body was settled into the sofa, but bent forward at the waist, and the long, bony, bent fingers of both of his hands were wrapped around a walking-stick between his knees as he watched another Delta sun go down.

CHAPTER VII

Processing

SEASONS IN the Delta are still marked in cotton time: someone will place an event chronologically by saying "it was around harvest time," or "cotton was about knee-high." Cotton is still the predominant vista and the sign of the season, a more precise calendar than the leaves on the trees or the temperature. Day by day, the landscape changes as the cotton grows from the lightest dusting of green breaking through the soil in early April to the explosion of white as the bolls open on the waist-high plants and are harvested from mid-September through October, after which the dry, dead stalks are left standing broken in the fields until spring, when they are ploughed under.

Cotton as a topic of conversation embraces many things, including the weather, the crop, equipment, hired help, the price on the market, and the fine points of the horrifically complicated government subsidy programs. All of these and many more aspects of cotton farming are frequent topics of conversation at the Pig Stand in Belzoni, or Mike and Sam's in Indianola. The Delta is still cotton country in a big way, and in 1989 about eighty-nine thousand acres of cotton were grown in Sunflower County, worth an estimated $39 million.

There is farm equipment on every road, in town and out. Tractors pull the massive wheeled implements that are used to farm cotton: diskers with their steel insect wings folded up into the air behind them, and eight-row cultivators that cover the shoulder of the road and half the highway. The farm implements impede traffic and slow it down, forming bottlenecks all up and down Highway 49. Anywhere along its length, from Clarksdale to Yazoo City, it is not unusual to find yourself poking along behind farm machinery, waiting for a chance to pass.

Eight-row cultivators are pulled down the rows by a tractor, turning up weeds with their tines and laying down herbicides in the broken soil through hoses. Such a cultivator will often put down four hundred gallons of chemicals a day, and does the chopping of about twenty adults working "can to can't," with the tractor driver the only employee needed to run it. Once the cost of fuel, herbicides, and pesticides are factored in, much of the cost effectiveness disappears, but the cultivators are still cheaper than hired help, and farmers do not have the labor headaches.

There are still particular times during the season when some farmers prefer using people with long-handled hoes to chop their cotton, rather than cultivators. A hoe can get up close to the young cotton, can reach places where the mechanical cultivator is not delicate enough to work without damaging the plants. Each day during those times, people who want work in the fields wait early in the morning at particular corners in the black neighborhoods. A labor

boss makes a contract and comes by the corner with a school bus to pick the people up and take them to the fields. At the end of the day they are paid less than thirty dollars, but it is more than they would earn otherwise. When I was out early, driving through the country, I occasionally passed one of those school buses parked by a field, disgorging its passengers, who walked in no great hurry out to a day chopping cotton, heads covered with hats or colorful bandanas against the fierce sun, hands curled around hoe handles, balancing them over shoulders like rifles, their other hands down by their sides holding water jugs.

A day spent chopping weeds from around cotton is not a whole lot different than a day spent cutting catfish, as people who have done both like to say, but the headgear is different: no bandanas, hats, or caps are allowed on the floor of the processing plants, only a hair net, which everyone is required to wear. Even visitors are required to don them as soon as they come into a plant. Companies order the white, disposable hair nets by the box load, and they show up all over town protecting people's hair-dos. Another item that travels beyond the walls of the plant is the tool of the trade—the deadly sharp filet knife. It leaves the plant in pockets, in boots, in purses. What goes easily through catfish meat also slides through human flesh without any problem, and filet knives occasionally turn up as the weapon of choice in violent assault cases.

Other parts of the uniform are left at the plants. These are things like the white lab coats, worn by all workers; the rubber boots for standing all day on cold, wet cement; the Kevlar "cut-resistant" glove worn at the filet table; and the even stronger stainless steel mesh glove worn by the women who are "headers."

Decapitation of the catfish is done by picking up a stunned, slippery fish from a conveyor belt and running it up against a vertical bandsaw, which slices off its head. Then the rest of the fish travels on down the kill line. The saw blade can cut through a finger as easily as a fish head, and can even cut through the mesh gloves, but the gloves slow the blade down enough so that the header usually has

enough time to jerk her hand away and not lose a fingertip. A good header loses none of the meat behind the head and is able to decapitate fifteen catfish a minute.

The Delta Pride plant in Indianola—the largest catfish processing facility in the world—is able to move through six hundred thousand pounds of fish a day if need be, although the plant's average daily output is less than half of that. Despite killing all of those fish each day, the plant has an aura of basic cleanliness, with only a slight fish odor in the air. The floors are concrete, wet from being regularly hosed down. The walls are tiled, and the noise level of the machinery is high, but not unbearable. Men drive forklifts back and forth, moving big aluminum tubs the size of laundry carts, packed with ice and fish, to the fileting tables, carrying fileted strips of meat to be frozen, and stacking pallets with wrapped tray-packs of catfish ready for the supermarket. The plant is in constant motion, with tow-motors gliding across the cement floor under bright-white fluorescent lighting.

The presence of nearby processing plants to handle a farmer's fish production was an early key to the growth of the catfish industry. In the late 1960s and through the 1970s, catfish were mostly transported on ice to live-fish markets in places like New Orleans, Houston, Atlanta, Chicago, and Detroit. Many of the farmers allowed the public to fish in their ponds and pay a per-pound price for what they caught, in an effort to keep the ponds thinned out. It wasn't until the product could be frozen and shipped that the industry was able to really expand, and this required processing plants.

The first plants were built by multinational corporations with a taste for investing in agricultural commodities. Con-Agra, Hormel, and Prudential Insurance marketed catfish under the respective labels of Country Skillet, Farm Fresh, and Wellfed. It took the farmers a while to catch on, but by 1981 they had an agricultural cooperative

put together, and Delta Pride began operations. There were excess fish that the existing plants did not want to buy, so Delta Pride never lacked product to be processed. The company rapidly carved out a share of the market, and enjoyed a 30 percent annual growth rate through 1986, when things began to slow down. Hormel and Con-Agra grew as well, although Prudential's Wellfed, the third multinational player, closed down in 1985 after a prolonged and bitter labor dispute. Delta Pride bought the Wellfed plant in Isola.

The growth of the processors' profits slowed down as their success spawned imitators. For about $2 million, a group of farmers could get a plant off the ground and running, and a lot of people watched Delta Pride's numbers and figured they could do as well themselves. By 1990, there were fifteen processing plants within a forty-mile radius of Belzoni, and most of the new ones were farmer-owned coops. Not many of them found it as lucrative as they had anticipated. It was hard to find markets where new brands would sell well, because other processors were already established.

The restaurants, food wholesalers, and supermarkets for many states around were already buying from one of the big three in 1990: Delta Pride, Con-Agra, or Hormel. Delta Pride had about 35 percent of all the sales. Next came the two multinationals: Con-Agra, with $12 billion in annual sales and ranking 35 on the Fortune 500 list of top-earning corporations, and Hormel, the world's largest producer of pork products. Between their two products, Country Skillet and Farm Fresh, they accounted for another 35 percent of catfish sales. With the big three accounting for 70 percent of all Delta catfish sold, the other dozen processing plants had to divide up the remaining 30 percent of the market, or be able to open and sell new territories.

When a farmer has on-flavor fish ready to go to the processing plant, a date and time is set for the fish to be harvested. The pond is

seined as closely as possible to the scheduled arrival of the live-haul truck from the plant. The primary tool for seining a catfish pond is around 1,200 feet of seine net, which costs about four dollars a foot. Seining also requires a couple of tractors, which any farmer is bound to have already, a little aluminum boat with a small outboard motor, and a crew of five or six.

The net is wrapped around a big steel spool, about the size of those wooden ones used to hold telephone wire. This is mounted on two wheels and is pulled along the levee behind a tractor. The net is paid off the spool and stretches across the pond to another tractor on the other side. There are corks on the top and lead weights along the bottom so that it stands up and creates a moveable fence in the water. The two tractors, one on either side of the pond, are driven slowly down the levees, pulling the net through the water, while the crew wades behind it, wearing chest-waders in the four-foot depths, and pushes the net along. The motorboat stays behind the net, nudging it here and there so that it stays abreast of the tractors. It takes at least an hour to seine a pond.

The middle of the seine net is shaped like a short funnel, which leads to a second, smaller net called a sock. As the seine moves forward, the fish in front of it swim along its length, looking for a hole. They swim through the funnel and into the sock. There are several sizes of socks with holes of various widths in their mesh, and they are used depending on the size of fish that the processing plant wants for the orders it is filling.

It looks like a fairly simple operation to seine a pond, but it represents a great technological evolution from the early days of catfish farming. "In 1968, we were getting thirty-five cents a pound for them, and we didn't know nothing about how to do anything," said one Isola farmer. "We learned by trial and error. We harvested with a dip net and a sorting platform, which was turned up at the edges to hold the fish on it, and had holes for the water to run out. We'd dip those fish up on the platform and go through them by hand."

Anyone who has had the pleasure of wading through a creek or

pond with a seine net, marveling at the variety of aquatic life that turns up, may think that working on a seining crew would be more pleasant than other minimum-wage jobs like working in a fast-food restaurant or chopping cotton, particularly on a mild, breezy, sunny morning in April like the one when I went out to watch Larry Cochran's crew seine a pond. He keeps a full-time seining crew, which works his ponds and those of seven other farmers who pay him for the service. The going rate is three cents for each pound of fish seined, and there is enough work to keep the crew busy all year, except for those few days in the dead of winter when there might be a thin film of ice on the ponds.

It turns out that making a living wading through a pond is not all that pleasant. An hour walking through four feet of water under a broiling Mississippi summer sun, or in the face of a winter wind coming across the surface of cold water is, in fact, no fun at all. An additional worry, particularly during the warmer months, is the ubiquitous water moccasin, which is found on the banks and occasionally encountered in the pond, as are water snakes, brown snakes, and snapping turtles.

Nevertheless, there is not a lot of work available in the Delta, and Larry Cochran's crew pretty much stays the same, with little turnover from year to year, according to James "Redbug" Sykes, Cochran's manager, a short, balding, slightly florid man. "These are good boys and they work pretty hard. I've got more or less the same crew we had last year and the year before that."

Sykes and his crew took eight thousand pounds of catfish out of the eleven-acre pond I watched them seine, amounting to about five thousand fish. When the tractors had brought the net the length of the pond, it was slowly wound back up on its spool, positioned on the pond bank. The trapped fish were herded into the middle of the net through the funnel and into the sock. Then the sock was quickly detached from the rest of the net and raised up on a half-dozen steel stakes driven into the bottom of the pond and extending a foot above the surface. The belly of the net remained underwater, with its

edges secured at the top of the stakes. It was a giant string bag, holding about four tons of fish imprisoned in the water until Delta Pride's live-haul truck arrived.

The crew then broke for lunch, stripping off their waders and standing around the back of Sykes's pickup with the makings for lunch on the back of the lowered tailgate: two loaves of white bread, an open jar of mayonnaise with a dinner knife stuck in it, and a package of bologna with enough meat for two sandwiches apiece. Each man got to reach in a big, economy-size bag of chips as it came around, and there were cold Cokes for everyone. I had a sandwich with a Coke. The day was warm and the levee was dusty. The members of the seining crew ate voraciously, then flopped down on the pond bank and stretched out to wait for the Delta Pride truck. Sykes put his tailgate up and drove off, returning a few minutes later behind the wheel of a three-quarter-ton pickup with an iron boom mounted on its bed. On the far end of the boom was a chain, from which hung a large, wire basket. A small, round grocer's scale hung from the chain above the basket.

Once the Delta Pride truck arrived and was positioned rear-to-rear with the pickup, it took the crew about twenty minutes to transfer eight thousand pounds of catfish from the sock to the truck. A live-haul truck is nothing more than a long, flat-bed trailer, with a big, stainless steel tank on it. The tank is divided into eight compartments, a trap door on each, and the compartments are half-full of water. Live-haul trucks are almost as common as tractors on the two lanes of Highway 49, but they do not poke along and hold up traffic. In fact, many a live-haul truck passed my van in a rush of noise and reflected light, gone hell-for-leather down the road.

The boom on Sykes's truck swung out over the pond, and two men in waders worked the sock. They grabbed hold of the heavy, huge basket and dipped it into the net, then the boom swung it back up, full of hundreds of pounds of writhing catfish, over to the live-haul truck, where it was positioned over an open trap door. Sykes perched up next to the trap doors and peered at the scale. He wrote

down the weight, then kicked a foot lever at the bottom of the basket, which opened it, dumping a cascade of fish with a watery roar
into the truck, ready for the journey to the processing plant.

The fish, of course, knew by that point that it was not an ordinary
day. Panic spread rapidly through the fish left in the sock as the basket dipped and dipped again. The spool slowly wound the net up on
the bank as the fish were herded closer and closer to the center of the
sock. The water in the net boiled.

When the fish reach the Delta Pride plant, they will be transferred
to another basket and weighed again. The farmer is paid according
to the weight at the plant, not the pond bank, and farmers say it is
common for weights at the plant to be a few hundred pounds lower
than when they loaded the fish at the pond bank, saving the processor, maybe, $375 on a load worth a total of $6,000. Farmers complain about the weight discrepancies, but not too much, and their
complaints are usually accompanied with a what-are-you-gonna-do
shrug of the shoulders. They need the continuing good will of a processing plant. Even if they own part of its stock, they want to be able
to count on fast action from the plant in a crisis, such as getting out
to harvest a pond quickly if fish begin turning up with hamburger
gill, getting as many as possible out before they die. If a farmer can
count on that kind of cooperation from a plant, there is no point in
complaining too much over a few hundred dollars at the scales.

After being weighed at the plant, the catfish are put in a large
holding tank, just outside the plant's wall. This is the last water in
which they will ever swim. When the assembly line is ready for
them, they are stunned with an electric charge, dipped out with yet
another wire basket, and dumped into chutes leading into the plant,
down to the killing floor. As they come out of the hopper inside the
Delta Pride plant, an automated gate directs them to one of fourteen
processing lines and, in short order, they are decapitated, eviscer-
ated, and skinned.

The bandsaws used to behead the fish are vertical blades that are
positioned just beside the belt, so the fish can be pushed against the

blade and, headless, continue right on down the line to one of two "rippers," whose job is to slice the fish from the anus to the top of the belly, exposing the entrails. Next is the eviscerating station, where an eviscerator is stuck in the open fish and sucks the guts out. A skinner then runs the fish over a set of whirring blades, flips it over, and does the other side in two quick movements. In less than a minute after coming out of the hopper, the fish is a clean piece of meat. It then spends fifteen minutes in an ice-water bath before being sent to be turned into filets, nuggets, strips, or packed whole catfish, depending on what orders are being filled.

Many of the jobs in the Delta Pride plant come with quotas attached. A header has to cut off fifteen heads a minute, and a fileter is required to cut eight hundred pounds of filets a day. Workers are allowed a five-minute bathroom break in the morning, and one fifteen-minute coffee break. Otherwise, they are expected to make their quotas, standing on the kill line or at the cutting table, working hard and fast. There is a roving crew that does nothing but sharpen knives all day, and still workers complain that they too frequently have to cut fish with dull knives.

There are plenty of other occupational hazards as well. Besides an accidental knife wound, or getting somehow caught in the machinery, there is carpal tunnel syndrome, also known as repetitive motion injury. Carpal tunnel often begins as a sensation of numbness along the hand and up the arm to the shoulder. It progresses into a chronic, debilitating pain for which there is no relief other than a nasty little piece of surgery usually performed on the nerve at the base of the hand and top of the wrist. It is a deep incision and takes a while to heal. A sizeable number of Delta Pride's workers have suffered from carpal tunnel syndrome.

Rosa Walker's story was typical: She worked eight years standing on the concrete floor at a long, stainless steel filet table, cutting cat-

fish with twenty-four other black women. In 1989, when Delta Pride's personnel manager told her she no longer had a job at the plant, she had already been through surgery on her right hand, her cutting hand, for which the company's insurance paid. When she came back to work, she was told there was no "light" work for her and was fired.

"They hire you, cripple you, and fire you out at Delta Pride," she told me bitterly. "They treat people like dogs out there. It's like being back on the plantation."

The United Food and Commercial Workers Union (UFCW) has organized a number of the plants. The organizing campaigns are hard-fought, and the union's victories come at the expense of long struggles. Some of the victories have been pyhrric, when management has bowed to the inevitable, but chosen to crash and burn the company before allowing unionization. When Mississippi companies lose battles with unions, they have a history of packing up and going out of state, finding other places where Third World conditions allow them to work people very hard while paying them very little. Mississippi is notoriously union-shy, and labor organizing is generally considered a slightly less respectable profession than pimping one's own children.

The UFCW's first big confrontation was at the Wellfed plant, owned by Prudential, just outside of Isola. It was the site of the first union election at a processing plant, and 108 of Wellfed's 144 non-supervisory employees, all of them black women, voted for UFCW representation. In time-honored Delta tradition, the company responded to the union's demand for a negotiated contract by totally ignoring it. Employees went out on strike, and the company replaced them with nonunion labor. After years of inconclusive court hearings, the company filed for bankruptcy, and the plant was bought by Delta Pride to serve as a satellite to its Indianola plant.

The union began trying to organize Delta Pride in 1986. In January, a mailing was sent out to many Delta Pride employees, which included authorization cards for a union-organizing effort to begin.

These requests for representation are the first step in an organizing effort. One of the first people to commit to the UFCW was Mary Young. Her mother had gotten a mailing, and she filled in a card and sent it back.

"I went to work in '83 and worked for Delta Pride four and a half years. It was pure-dee hell. I was working the kill line. No matter what the reason—you could be sick, or your child could be sick, and you could carry in a doctor's statement—if you took off work you might get fired. They'd tell you to your face, 'I don't care if your mama's sick, you better be here on this job, or else don't you come back.' They'd talk to you any kind of way, and whatever happened you could suffer it or leave. It was terrible. I figured things couldn't get any worse, so I sent in the union card."

Young is short and compact, with a quick-flashing gold-toothed smile, rough hands that have known hard work, and a determined gleam in her eyes. It was not long before she was handing out authorization cards to her fellow workers. Delta Pride fought the organizing efforts tooth and nail.

"They fired about twenty people. If you had a mother or a sister or a brother working out there, they'd call them in and tell them if they messed around with the union they'd get fired. Anyone they thought might have any union activities was gone, although they never fired me. They harassed people every day about it. But all those people who got fired won their cases and they're either back at work or took a settlement."

The union won the election and the right to represent Delta Pride workers in negotiations. In June 1987, the company and UFCW Local 1529 signed a three-year contract. It did not go far toward bettering either wages or benefits for the plant workers, but the union reasoned that it was a foot in the door. The UFCW bought its local a small, one-story office building in downtown Indianola, just across an alley from the law offices of the mayor, Tommy McWilliams, who also happened to be Delta Pride's attorney. By 1990, six other plants in the Delta were successfully organized, including Con-

Agra's Country Skillet and Hormel's Farm Fresh, despite the fact that during the same period Hormel was involved in a bitter strike at its meat-packing plants in Minnesota. Young was named as the union's representative, and she was the person charged with monitoring compliance with the contracts. She opens the office each morning, then spends most of the rest of her day driving between the six catfish plants, collecting grievances, and meeting with union members and personnel managers.

"Delta Pride is the worst, they have simply not lived up to the contract," Young told me in the spring of 1990. "The other plants are different. Farm Fresh and Country Skillet are places where you can sit down and talk about a problem, but at Delta Pride you always have to file a grievance on it."

In addition, Young said, Delta Pride was particularly reluctant to address the problem of carpal tunnel syndrome, either by reducing production quotas or exploring rotation systems for workers, designed to keep them changing jobs and motions. A committee had been established at Con-Agra to deal with carpal tunnel syndrome and make suggestions for keeping its incidence low at the plant. Officials there were sensitive to the problem and were attempting to deal with it, according to Young. Not so at Delta Pride. The federal Occupational Safety and Health Administration carried out inspections of Delta Pride's plants between June and November 1989, and found twenty-five violations of law, including a number of serious and willful violations. Among the violations OSHA cited were an absence of safeguards against cumulative trauma disorders, which include carpal tunnel syndrome and tendonitis. OSHA charged that there were no engineering or administrative controls to reduce risk of cumulative trauma disorders; improper medical management including failure to treat injuries promptly; and a failure to maintain required logs of injuries and illnesses. OSHA levied penalties of $32,800. Delta Pride immediately appealed the OSHA decision, and after a protracted period of hearings, an agreement was reached in 1991 between the company and the agency. OSHA reduced the

seriousness of the violations and Delta Pride paid fines totaling $12,500.

By 1990, it had begun to appear that Delta Pride not only bought the Wellfed plant when Prudential abandoned it, but was committed to carrying on the intransigent attitude toward the union that had done so much to close it down. Sam Hinote, president of Delta Pride Catfish, Inc., and Turner Arant, chair of the board, were vocal in their hostility toward the union, particularly as profits flattened out in the face of increased competition. The 1987 union contract expired in June 1990, and in late August of that year the company gave the union its "final" offer: a six-percent per year raise and a one-percent increase in pension contributions. The company would not budge from that offer, refusing, in effect, to negotiate.

"We have given the best offer we can make without compromising the financial integrity of our company," said a Delta Pride representative.

Union members rejected the offer, and, on September 7, nine hundred of them walked out and began a strike. The company immediately began hiring replacement workers to cross the picket line. There were violent incidents on both sides of the line during the course of the thirteen-week strike. The union alleged that a company supervisor threatened strikers with a gun, and Delta Pride accused picketers of assaulting those who crossed the picket line to work.

An Indianola catfish farmer named Winford "Red" Austin, who ran a very high-stakes poker game in his home for many years, was indicted along with his son, an attorney, for offering a $5,000 bribe to a worker on the union's bargaining committee, if she would speak out for ending the strike. Federal charges were brought against them. Neither side denied that the bribery attempt took place, because the offers had been taped, but Austin's defense attorneys held that the Austins had not violated the Taft-Hartley Act, which prohibits employers from interfering with a strike. The indictment was dismissed by a federal judge, who agreed with the defense that the

two men were acting on their own and not on behalf of Delta Pride, even though the Austins had 1,500 acres under water and were Delta Pride shareholders.

Jobs were scarce in the Delta, and increasing numbers of people were hired as replacement workers for the strikers. The company called them replacement workers, but the picketers called them scabs. Delta Pride's production was definitely slowed by the strike, but it was not halted. The company issued a series of business-as-usual press releases and seemed to be well positioned for a protracted strike.

Then the momentum began to shift toward the UFCW. The union called for a national boycott of Delta Pride's product. Negotiations were opened for new contracts with Con-Agra and Hormel, negotiations that quickly bore fruit. Many of the striking Delta Pride workers were hired at Con-Agra, which negotiated another three-year contract with the union in a month of agreeable bargaining. The company had not done so badly either in the new contract, agreeing to a first-year average wage of $4.87 an hour by 1993. There were some on the Delta Pride board who looked at that and wondered if it wouldn't be easier and cheaper, in the long run, to sign a new contract.

The boycott of Delta Pride products immediately drew the support of the Atlanta-based Southern Christian Leadership Conference, and its president Joseph Lowery came to Indianola for a rally. Jesse Jackson sent a letter of support: "Your cause is generating more than sympathy; it is generating anger against those who have turned a plant into a plantation. That anger will be heard resoundingly at checkout counters across America ringing up 'no sale' on Delta Pride products."

The strike began to garner some attention in the national press, where it was portrayed as a civil rights issue. Then Turner Arant made a mistake. In early November, the "Today" show aired a weekday morning news piece about the strike, which showed Arant walking around his ponds, discoursing in baronial fashion, proudly

showing the camera crew through his huge home, and avowing that catfish had been good to him. These scenes were intercut with a Delta Pride worker, out on strike, who also proudly displayed her small, neat home on the south side of the tracks for the camera and talked about how her pay at the plant did not leave her with anything at the end of the month after she put food on the table for her eight family members.

Delta Pride's board of directors was furious with Arant for having been made to look like an unfeeling fat cat. He resigned at a special meeting soon after the show aired and was replaced with a man named Harold Potter, who union officials immediately hailed as much more reasonable. Negotiations with the union were resumed, and on December 13, a contract was agreed to, which raised beginning wages to ten cents over minimum wage and paid a minimum of $4.75 to anyone with a year's experience. Delta Pride also agreed to institute a safety committee and expand its "human relations" program.

A real change in the human relations between workers and management within the plant walls of Indianola's largest employer might, indeed, make some difference. The ideas about human relations that are held by most Indianolans could do with some changing. The untouching, parallel lives of black and white Deltans need to be merged and the processing plants could set that example although they do not show much inclination to do so. Some real human relations in the Delta might eventually make for a decent place to have a drink.

My taste in drinking establishments runs to places where some of the drinkers are old, all races are welcomed, the music is not too loud, and a lot of stories get traded back and forth across the bar. It was a hard taste to satisfy in Indianola. On the black side of town

the choice is between the Club Ebony, a long, large, and lovely nightclub with a stage and a cover charge on weekends, or the juke joints down along "the flats," a three-block stretch by the railroad tracks. At either one, I would be the lone white person in the place, which sometimes made it hard to relax in anonymity at the bar, although the Club Ebony was friendly enough, owned by Mary Shepherd, an influential woman in the black community, kind and honorable. It was a pleasant club, and while I was not made to feel particularly welcome by the other patrons, I was not likely to be confronted or hassled at the bar.

There was no such assurance if I went into the jukes. There was no telling what might happen in one of those strange clubs with a tin roof thrown over a few old card tables on a cement floor and a rickety bar, all of which had probably been there for fifty years under one or another name. The walls are often drawn or written on, always with a jukebox in one corner, gleaming and colorful, chock-a-block with music by the likes of Tyrone Davis, Little Milton, B. B. King and Bobby Bland, the deep-soul favorites of the Delta. In the juke joints, particularly on the weekends, spirits are high and flaring, people drink to forget their troubles and let themselves go, and it is tough to be a white guy sitting quietly at the bar listening to music.

Once when I was in a juke, sitting at the bar with a beer in front of me, waiting for the band to come on, I was accosted by a big, broad guy with a goatee and a glare, dressed in a green hospital surgical shirt and jeans. He crossed the room to put four quarters in the big Seeburg jukebox, trimmed in red neon, and, as he turned back toward his table, his eye caught mine and in a flash he was beside me at the bar and right up in my face.

"Why don't you just go on back to Cuba?" he said, in a loud, menacing voice, mistaking my dark complexion for Hispanic. "Get your funky ass back to Cuba."

At first I couldn't understand what he was saying because he had a thick Delta accent slurred further by whiskey, but there was no

mistaking the raw anger and animosity in his voice, so I listened up. "Get on back there, what you have to come here for, go on back to Cuba and take your damned family with you."

The group I was waiting to hear was a blues aggregate from Greenville that I really wanted to catch, but this guy showed no sign of letting up. I started to try and tell him I was not from Cuba, but he just kept hollering and cursing me. Then I made the mistake of waiting until he stopped for breath and telling him that at least in Cuba white and black people could drink at the same bar, go to school together, and get free medical treatment. He turned up his harangue a notch and it looked uncomfortably close to the point where he would try throwing me back to Havana. I drained the beer as fast as I could and skedaddled home, my tail between my legs, blues group unheard.

As far as white bars go, there is Chevy's on the north side of Indianola, right out on Highway 82. This is a place with a young drinking crowd, loud and indiscreet, pool tables you put a quarter in, and a country-rock band on the weekends. People stop off there driving between Greenwood in the east and Greenville in the west, drinking their way across the Delta. This was not a place I enjoyed taking an evening's glass or two, so I was usually left with the pool room downtown.

Pool rooms, on both the black and white sides of town, represent a long tradition in the Delta. They are places where men gather to play cards, or pool, or dominos, and to drink. Respectable women would not be seen in a pool room. They take their evening's entertainment in each other's homes or at the country club. Even among men the pool rooms are a dying institution, as television, videotapes, and bars like Chevy's claim a larger and larger share of the young trade, and the old customers die out. Indianola's white pool room downtown has been there since at least 1906, according to its present owner, Gene Shelton, and the five pool tables in the place look like they could have been constructed then. They are broad, sturdy,

thick-legged tables made out of heavy, dark wood. The business license on the wall behind the bar is made out to The Indianola Domino Club, but everyone in town calls the place either "Gene's" or "the pool room."

In the back there is, in fact, a domino table and it is frequently occupied. It has a plexiglass top, and when the dominos are laid down they make a pleasing click you can hear up front by the bar. There are comfortable, old leather folding chairs built around the walls where people can sit and kibbitz the pool games. Shelton started working in the place in 1958, and bought it in 1962. He has a chair behind one end of the bar, a comfortable, cracked-leather, swivel easy chair, which is tilted back in a permanent lean. Gene is short and squat, and when he is settled in his chair, his feet are off the floor. In the evenings he keeps an oversize plastic mug on a shelf beside him. The mug is large enough to easily hold a bottle of Budweiser, and he refills it at regular intervals.

One evening I was standing on the sidewalk in front of Gene's talking to Jim Abbott, editor of the *Enterprise-Tocsin*. It was about 8 P.M. and the streets were deserted. A car pulled up to the curb beside us, a Cadillac, and a middle-aged woman behind the wheel lowered the window on the passenger side with a push-button. "Excuse me," she said to Jim. "Do you know my son?"

"Yes," he said, and spoke her son's name.

"Would you go in and see if he's in there, and if he is tell him his mama's outside?" she asked him, nodding her head toward Gene's. "I've never set foot in a pool hall in my life."

Mothers could not call the pool room looking for their sons, nor wives looking for their husbands. Gene refused to get a telephone, because if he did, he said, people would always be calling and looking for one of his regulars. "We wouldn't get no peace," he said, leaning back in his chair.

The pool hall door is always locked, and to get in a customer knocks on it. Gene has a buzzer mounted on the wall, within arm's

length of his chair, so he can reach over and buzz a person in. It is not hard to imagine who he wants to keep out. There is probably not a white man in the state he would not sell a beer to.

One Wednesday night in the pool room someone said, "Let's go out to Red's and play some cards," which occasioned a lot of laughing at the bar. Gene chuckled.

"Sounds good to me," I said. I like to play cards for a little money from time to time.

Gene leaned back in his chair and clued me in: "You can't even sit down out at Red Austin's with less than a few thousand in your pocket."

On a Wednesday night? Seven nights a week, he told me.

Are these local people playing cards for these stakes seven nights a week? Yep, said Gene.

There was often $150,000 a night changing hands in Red Austin's house, according to the FBI agents who swooped down on the house one spring night in 1990, carting off forty people and over $200,000 in cash. Big-stakes games had gone on for nearly ten years in Austin's brick home, and everyone in Indianola knew it. In fact, the games were not entirely local. People came fairly long distances to gamble at Austin's. Over the years, the sheriff and the police chief had been questioned by the *Enterprise-Tocsin* about the game, and both maintained that as soon as they got one complaint about it, they would pursue an investigation, but no one ever complained.

No wonder—Austin had some large men working for him. When they weren't looking out for his other interests, some of those large men worked at Austin's catfish ponds. The FBI announced it was investigating to determine if gambling revenues had financed his 1,500 acres of ponds and whether the government could seize them under racketeering statutes. They decided against it. After his arrest, the sixty-one-year-old Austin pled guilty, pledging to cooperate with federal officials investigating gambling in northern Mississippi, and was given a lenient fifteen-month sentence.

"I miss the old days," said Gene, commenting on Austin's arrest,

as he dumped a bottle of Bud into his mug and shook in some salt on top of it. "You know, liquor only got legal here in 1968. I liked it better the other way. There's four liquor stores in town right now, and the same four guys that own them used to bootleg, right in those same places, but in those days you could wake them up any time, they didn't mind. They were always glad to roll out of bed and sell you a bottle. Now it's strictly ten to ten. If you're late, you can forget it. In the old days, the bootleggers paid the sheriff two dollars a case, as well as paying a revenue tax to the state, even though selling it wasn't legal. Everybody knew where everybody else stood. Those were the days."

CHAPTER VIII

Delta Ancestors

THERE IS a history of black Deltan landowners, farming families, with roots in Delta soil that go as far back as the whitest of Deltans, on land bought in the aftermath of the Civil War. Grandparents passed it on to their children, and they passed it on to their daughters and sons.

About five miles northwest of Indianola is an unincorporated area named Stephenville. It was cleared and settled in 1873 by a group of about thirty ex-slaves from Alabama who arrived in covered wagons and were led by a family named Stephens. Much of the land was owned by a Quaker who lived in Texas, and he was glad to sell it to the settlers for about three dollars an acre, according to Sunflower

County's preeminent local historian, Marie Hemphill, in her county history, *Fevers, Floods and Faith.*

The Alabama families settled in and did just what their white counterparts were doing. They built a sawmill and cleared the land, using the first trees—almost always first-growth cypress—as timber for their houses, then selling a little of the rest and burning most of it. As soon as they could, they planted the cleared land in cotton. The Delta was no more hospitable to them than it was to white settlers. Malaria cut them down like wheat, and those who lived had their energies sapped by fevers, hard work, and isolation.

In 1976, Marie Hemphill interviewed an eighty-nine-year-old man named Clarence Dixon, who remembered his parents talking about how life had been at Stephenville during the early years. "The wolves would come up to the house and howl like dogs," Dixon told her. "The pig pens had to be walled up high and covered to keep the wolves and panthers out. Bears were a nuisance and a danger, too, and people were afraid to walk very far down the path away from the house."

In the late 1920s, there were over one hundred landowners in Stephenville, and it was a prosperous community supporting a number of businesses. But by 1955, all the businesses were gone and only fifty families were living in the area, and of those only six were landowners, according to Hemphill. A steady increase of mechanized farming meant there was less and less work for those who depended on work in the fields, and there were fewer and fewer farmers who could afford to keep working smaller parcels of land. People moved into town to look for work, or gave up and left altogether. By 1990, there were only a handful of people left with ties to the old community.

Mound Bayou, a town in Bolivar County thirty miles northwest of Indianola, was founded in 1887 by a group of ex-slaves, including people who had been owned by Joseph Davis, whose brother Jefferson Davis was president of the Confederacy. In 1907, Mound Bayou was a thriving town, with eight hundred residents owning thirty

thousand acres of land, but by the Depression things had slowed down considerably, and the town never recovered, beginning a long slide into a Third World poverty that persisted in 1990. Some of the citizens of Mound Bayou are hard-working farmers, descendants of the early settlers, freedmen who had brought a utopian sense of commitment and faith to the community. That faith still waits to be realized. Mound Bayou is desperately poor, bleak, in as bad shape, or worse, than the towns around it.

Most of the land still owned by black Delta farmers had been bought and cleared by their ancestors, but hard work has not proved to be enough to prosper with a farm, or even to hold on to it. Like their paler brethren, the black farmers who survived during the 1980s did so by being more than good farmers. They did it by endless scuffling, by carrying large debt-loads, and by mastering the byzantine federal crop subsidy programs. But, when it came to farming catfish, black farmers did not receive the same welcome at banks and lending institutions as white farmers.

"There are two black catfish farmers beside me that I know of in the state of Mississippi," Ed Scott, Jr. told me. He has eight ponds and is the owner of Pond Fresh Catfish, making him the only black owner of a catfish processing plant in the United States.

"Out of 335,000 acres under water, about 200 of them are owned by blacks. They can't get the money to get started. No one wants to lend that much to a black man. The banks won't lend money to a black farmer who wants to get into catfish."

Ed Scott's father, Ed Scott, Sr., also was a successful farmer. He had a sizeable piece of land outside Drew in northern Sunflower County, which he began amassing just before the Depression. "My father came here from Alabama in 1919 with $950 he had saved up. He worked as a sharecropper for about four years, then he went and rented some land and stayed there a while, and then he bought 101

acres. He would buy one piece of land, then another. When he died, the family owned 1,900 acres."

Drew is a tough town. Over the years, black people have been killed there for no other reason than the color of their skin. As recently as 1971, Jo Eatha Collier, eighteen, was shot as she walked down the street with her friends by a man who told the police he was just looking to shoot a black person. During the Freedom Summer of 1964, Drew had a reputation as a particularly intransigent town. It is the closest community to Parchman Farm, and many of its citizens work at the prison. Drew is not a prosperous town. Like most other Delta towns its size—about 2,500 people—it has a few wealthy planters, farmers, and *latifundistas*, but many people are struggling to get by, week to week. In Drew, financial security comes hard for a white person and twice as hard for a black person.

Nevertheless, Ed Scott's father had earned the begrudging respect of most of the town's residents, black and white. A good farmer is a good farmer, regardless of his race, and everyone in town knows what constitutes one. They concurred that Ed Scott, Sr. was hard-working and productive. He raised mostly cotton, although in 1948 he became the first black rice farmer in the state.

Ed Scott, Jr. followed in his father's footsteps on the family land and raised cotton, soybeans, and rice, just as his white neighbors were doing. And, like his father, he is a farmer of the Delta stripe, not afraid to take a risk. When he saw catfish farming pull some of his white neighbors back from the edge of financial disaster, where many of them were teetering along with farmers across the nation, he decided to dig some ponds and grow some fish.

A trip to see Scott's processing plant is a trip out into the country—*way* out into the country. "When you get to a raggedy little grocery, across the street from a school, turn right and keep going about six miles until the paved road runs out," he told me on the phone. "Then take the second dirt road to your right, and keep on 'til you see the plant."

That last road runs for a few dusty miles between cotton fields.

There is an occasional handwritten sign nailed to a fence post with POND FRESH lettered on it and an arrow to point the way. I passed an unplanted field, the remnants of the past year's cotton crop still in the ground. A hawk circled low over it, hunting rodents among the dry, brown cotton stalks. Finally the dirt road passed catfish ponds on the left and a small, well-kept plot of ground on the right, dotted with half a dozen tombstones. Just beyond the family cemetery was the Scott's brick home, and a little further beyond that the processing plant, where he has his office.

At sixty-eight, Ed Scott, Jr. is a rotund man whose standard dress is a pair of brown cotton work pants and a work shirt with his name stitched over one pocket. He has a cheerful face, a fringe of grey hair, and a deep, easy laugh. He is, by his own admission, an extremely independent-minded, stubborn man, and it is a good thing, too, or he would not have survived long enough to be named Mississippi Minority Businessman of 1989. He dug his ponds—eight of them—in 1981. It was not easy and he had not expected it to be.

"I'd been row-cropping right along, but I'm one of those versatile kind of farmers. Anything I see anybody else doing, I figure I can do it too. I started digging the ponds with my own equipment.

"The district supervisor from Farmer's Home Administration came out and saw me, and told me, 'You know I ain't going to let you have no money to pay for that dirt you're moving, don't you?' I went right on digging. When I was done I went to him and asked for a loan to stock them. He said no, and then he turned right around and let a white farmer I knew have five-and-a-half million dollars for catfish."

Scott was outraged and went over the supervisor's head to the state office in Jackson. There, they loaned him enough money to stock the ponds with 600,000 fingerlings and feed them for a few months.

"When I got that hundred and fifty thousand dollars from Farmer's Home, it was just enough to get me in trouble," he laughed. "As soon as I had those fish grown up to where I figured they were near

about ready for the market, I went looking for something to do with them, somewhere to process them. At that time, there weren't many places to process fish, and of course I didn't have stock in Delta Pride. When they were building a plant near here called Grain Fed in 1983, which had some government money in it, I went to the lawyer handling the paperwork and said I'd like to buy some stock. He said he'd get me some. The lawyer came back and told me straight up that because of the color of my skin he couldn't get me any stock. I said to myself, if the government will put money in that plant then they're no better than the white folks in Mississippi."

Scott decided he would go into the processing business for himself. He has told the story of how he did it on a videotape recorded for the Sunflower County library's extensive oral history project in 1989: "I said to my son, 'I'm not gonna let them stop me. Let's go on down to Indianola, go through one of those plants and see what it is they're doing that we can't do.' We went down to my lawyer's office in Indianola, and his secretary called Delta Pride and said she had two men who wanted to tour the plant and they said come on."

On the videotape, at this point in the story, Scott leans back in the chair behind his desk and laughs with great hilarity and satisfaction. "If she had said two black men wanted to see the plant, I don't think we would have gotten in, because when we walked in to tour the plant and they saw we were black, we sat there forty-five minutes before somebody said one word. Finally, Larry Steed, who was in charge of public relations, came out and got us.

"On the way through the plant, Larry Steed asked me, 'Y'all got a farm?' I said, 'Yep,' and kept walking. In a few minutes he asked if I had any stock in a plant, and I said, 'Nope.'

"He said, 'Well, what the hell you gonna do with your fish, then? Eat 'em yourself?'

"I said, 'Yep, something like that. I'm gonna see what you're doing I can't do, then I'm gonna clean my own fish.'"

Ed Scott told me how pleased he was that he told that story on videotape and that it was in the library for anyone to look at who

wanted to. Particularly pleased because he had done what he said he would. When he and his son returned home from Delta Pride, it did not take long to get a basic plant with one kill line built. He hired a friend of his from Drew, whom he described as the best carpenter in town, and together they turned Scott's tractor shed into a catfish processing plant. He struggled constantly with the ill-will and hostility of the white people around him, and that has not changed.

The written signs on the fenceposts showing visitors the way to the Pond Fresh plant have a short half-life, first riddled with bullets, then torn down and left to blow across the fields. If a lost truck driver, or salesperson, or journalist asks a white person in Drew where the plant is, a blank stare is likely to be the answer, then, perhaps, "Oh yeah, there was a colored fellow had a little ol' plant, but I don't think he's still in business."

That was much the same reaction I got from people in the catfish industry. They knew perfectly well who Ed Scott was and where he lived, but they would tell me, "Yeah, there used to be a colored fellow up near Drew ran some catfish . . . I heard he shut down. . . ."

Premature reports of the death of his plant are a part of life for Scott, and he shrugs them off. He has spent his adult years holding his head up and moving straight ahead, despite the obstacles thrown in his path, as his father did before him. "People here understand that they better know what they're doing when they bother me, because they know I'm gonna stand my ground if I'm right," he told me.

"My daddy was the same way. I'll never forget one time, in 1937, he bought a new Chevrolet truck. We had a lot of cars and trucks around. Shortly after we went to Vicksburg to move a family—we used to do that for work then if we had the time—and it wore out the tire on the right front, so he had me drive it down to the Chevrolet garage for them to check it and put another tire on it. One of the partners in the place named Frank started cussing me like a dog. I went home and told my daddy.

"He told me to go out and get in his car. He went and got his pis-

tol, put it in his hip pocket, went and got his Winchester and laid it on the back seat. He drove back to the garage with that Winchester on the back seat and his pistol in his pocket where people could see it sticking up under his coat. He walked into the garage and said, 'Mister Frank, Mister Bob, I'd like to see you in your office.'

"They knew Ed Scott was mad then. They got in there and he said, 'Look, I have eight vehicles and I can't drive them all at once. If I can't send my boy where he's gonna be treated right, I'll send my business somewhere else. Another thing I want you to know is that you don't cuss my children. I don't cuss 'em, and they ain't none of yours. From this day on I want you to know that if you kick one of Ed Scott's children, come kick Ed Scott. He's a little older and he can take it better.' I remember it like it was yesterday. My daddy didn't take no mess."

Ed Scott, Jr. is the same way and has been for a long time. "Back in the early 1960s, I went down in the evenings, carrying food to the first groups of Freedom Riders that came through here. They were camped out, and I drove food down to Belzoni, Louise, as far as Yazoo City. The highway patrol knew my tag number by heart. They would follow right along behind me."

Scott was a friend of Fannie Lou Hamer and her husband, Perry. Hamer, from Ruleville, just south of Drew, became a heroine of the civil rights movement. She founded the Mississippi Freedom Democratic Party, which was a strong third-party force in Mississippi during the movement years, and eventually opened up the regular Democratic Party to black citizens.

"Fannie Lou Hamer was the lady who first started the voter registration drive down here, and the man she worked for drove her off his place," Scott told me. "She was carrying his hoe hands to the fields and after she got through carrying them she went back and carried the cotton pickers. She kept the weights and times and all the records for him. She was a hard worker.

"One morning she went to the courthouse in Indianola to register. When she got back he met her and asked, 'Where you been?'

"She said, 'I been down there to register.'

"He said, 'Why you want to register? You ain't gonna vote. Ain't no niggers gonna vote here.' Just like that is how he said it. Then he said, 'Since you got so high and mighty as to register, I want you to move right now.' He was cutting off his nose to spite his face, because she was doing all of his work, plus carrying out his cotton pickers and cotton choppers.

"So she moved into Drew and started preaching, and she told the truth." Scott swung back in his wooden desk chair, laughing, eyes dancing. "Yes, she really did. I knew her and I knew her well. Both her and her husband. She used to live right down the road a little piece and she was really something."

Perhaps if Fannie Lou Hamer had lived long enough—she died in 1978—she might have gone into catfish farming like Ed Scott. She did organize a short-lived cooperative farm experiment in Ruleville. Hamer traveled widely across the United States on speaking tours before she died, and spent time in Washington, D.C., testifying before Congress and lobbying for civil rights. She had the kind of hard-headed persistence that would have made for a pretty good catfish farmer.

There was nothing easy about getting a processing plant for Ed Scott. He did not have the clout at the bank of a cooperative group of white Delta farmers. In fact, he had no clout at all. He had to build the plant on his own, bit by bit. He needed to cut corners to save money, but he was careful not to do anything that would make the plant fail to meet industry standards. When the plant was finished, he wrote Dr. McGill Berry in the food and fiber department of Mississippi State University, and asked him to come to Drew and inspect Pond Fresh's new one-line plant to see that it met health, safety, and quality standards.

"That was in 1985," he told me. "At that point we started skinning and processing by hand. From there, we upgraded our plant to what we have now: seven skinners on the line, four headsaws, eviscerators, and everything else any other plant has, and we've been in-

spected by the federal government and can sell to anybody we want."

By 1990, Scott's plant had expanded to two lines, compared to Delta Pride's fourteen, and he produced about 2 million pounds of catfish under the Pond Fresh label. That may seem like small potatoes when compared to Delta Pride's 140 million pounds a year, but it is enough to keep thirty-five employees working most of the time and some money coming in.

Scott taught himself the fine points of bidding on federal, state, and municipal contracts to provide catfish for the military's kitchens, a state office building's cafeteria, or a county's school system. Like all catfish processors, he struggles constantly with the market price of fish, both what he pays for them at the pond bank and the price he asks for them after they are processed; he also endures the seemingly endless number of things that can go wrong when you ship large loads of fish in refrigerated trucks to far-flung parts of the country.

Unlike his white competitors, to whom a long line of credit at a local bank is as critical to farming as a tractor, Scott works under the handicap of being *persona non grata* at local lending institutions. Nevertheless, the markets for Pond Fresh catfish have grown slowly, and as they do, he upgrades the plant, which in turn brings new customers. He has learned how to balance the local disadvantages of his minority status with its advantages at the federal level. He became a lay expert in the rules and regulations governing federal purchasing, and discovered, in the process, that he is eligible as a minority small-business owner to a 10 percent bid preference.

He began to win government contracts. Catfish was increasingly popular on military tables, for instance, sometimes served as often as once a week. Delta Pride also bid on government contracts, and after a while company officials took note of the Pond Fresh presence. At one point in 1987, both processors found themselves bidding on the same contract.

"That was a contract for fifty-five hundred pounds of filets. All

right. The government was letting big business bid against me. I bid at $2.89 a pound and they came in at $2.55. They figured I was getting that 10 percent, although the government never gave it to me, but Delta Pride was willing to bid that low, lose money, just to make sure I wouldn't get it."

Scott complained to Washington. He cited them chapter and verse from the regulations, which said that big business cannot bid in minority set-aside programs.

"The government stopped it immediately when they got my letter. They stopped the brokers and big business from bidding. That's when Delta Pride really got mad."

He leaned back in his chair and laughed. It was evident that he got a certain satisfaction out of being the David doing battle with Delta Pride's Goliath. It is a role he has known all his life, in one form or another, and which he saw his father live through before him. Ed Scott, Jr. and his wife, Edna, have raised five children and survived on their land with their family. They have guarded what was left them and made it through some tough times. Scott is gruff with his employees, keeping them busy and watching them closely. He is also someone who can be counted on for an advance if there is a family crisis, and who would not fire a woman for calling in at the last minute because her child was sick and she could not come to work. A job on Pond Fresh's kill line or at the filet table is not easy work, but it is also not Delta Pride, with its twenty minutes of bathroom breaks a week.

Another difference between Pond Fresh and Delta Pride is the company cafeteria. At Delta Pride there is a "lunch room" that amounts to a large locker room with iron picnic tables bolted to the floor, a microwave oven on a shelf, and a bunch of vending machines. At Pond Fresh, the cafeteria is a separate, one-story, cinder-block building across the parking lot from the processing plant, and it is under the dominion of Edna Scott, who is also the chef. She is a superb cook, and, as a company cafeteria, it is one in a million.

"This time lunch is on the house," Ed Scott told me as we walked

across the parking lot, the first time I ate there. "You can come back and see me around the middle of the day again, but next time you gotta buy your own lunch."

It was always a pleasure for me to do so, because for less than three dollars you get a plate of food as nourishing as it is ample: fresh sweet potatoes, turnip greens, and catfish fried in Edna Scott's secret batter, different from all the rest, she said, because of her special mix of ingredients.

In 1989, the Scotts joined forces with a Delta native named Robert Bush, who at that time was an aide in Washington to Mike Espy, Mississippi's first black congressman in this century. The Scotts, together with Bush, opened a restaurant in Washington called Edna's Gourmet Seafood, which includes catfish fried in thin jackets of her secret recipe. If that restaurant is any kin at all to the Pond Fresh cafeteria, Washingtonians are in luck.

Ed Scott is nagged by the worry that one day the other processors might decide to put him out of business and convince the farmers not to sell him fish, leaving him with nothing to market. So far, green has been the color to carry the most weight, people selling him fish because of his money, not his skin. Still, he does not rest easy. "To see, like I have, the extremes to which white people will go, and how much money they will spend to keep a black person down, it makes you think. It really does."

In the Delta, race is never far from anyone's thoughts. A remarkable number of conversations touch on it, even between people overheard talking casually in restaurants or bars. The catfish farmers in the Pig Stand, for instance, will work their way around a conversational route that covers cotton and catfish, but many of the stories they tell have outright or implicit racial themes. The black waitress at the Pig Stand seems oblivious to the conversations of the white farmers around the tables, perched on their drugstore stools, and

their frequent derogatory allusions to her race. White Deltans have an endless fund of stories about black Deltans, stories told as if they were the funniest little ol' thing ever heard, but which are not funny at all, serving only to express contempt for the Delta's African-Americans.

One night I was in the home of one of Indianola's old heads, a retired Sunflower County official, and we were sitting at the dinner table. He was telling after-dinner stories while his wife came in and out, clearing away the dishes and coming back in with pie and coffee.

"Folks just don't understand the colored people here like we do," he opined. "Look, I remember one afternoon my Willy, who'd been out on our farm forever, came into town trying to find me. I wasn't home, but my wife was. 'Is something wrong?' she asked him, when he showed up at the back door. He said, 'My baby died. He was okay when I left home this morning, sucking on titty and eating oatmeal, then when I came home midday for dinner he was dead.'"

As I contemplated the image of the stricken father and the limp, lifeless child, the old head leaned back in his chair and laughed, joined by the chuckling of his wife who was bringing the pie in from the kitchen. "Now you know I'd never say 'titty' to a woman, but it doesn't mean anything to these colored," he said, shaking his head.

It was odd that in a place where this kind of ugly anecdote is common as dirt, other kinds of ethnic differences matter less than in many American towns and cities. Go figure: the Indianola Country Club accepts Jews and Gentiles alike, and country clubs are the second most important social institutions in the Delta after churches. Jewish and Asian children may, and do, attend Indianola Academy, and Jews and Chinese have roots in the Delta as deep as blacks and whites.

There have been Chinese in the Delta since 1867, when the first Chinese laborers were shipped in from Cuba to see how they would do as replacements for the recently emancipated slaves. Everything Delta planters had heard about "coolie" labor building railroads in

the West made it sound like the Chinese might fit the bill. Word also spread among the Chinese in California that there was work in Mississippi clearing and planting land, and a number of them made the journey. The Chinese were treated as black when they arrived, and were subject to Jim Crow laws. They generally lived in bachelor societies, because for many years Chinese women were prohibited by law from immigrating to the United States.

When the men saved enough from their labors, they opened small grocery stores, and that is how the Chinese prospered in the Delta. They owned groceries in the middle of little towns, primarily serving a black clientele. The markets still exist today, in smaller numbers, with the judicious extension of credit as an incentive to keep people from doing their shopping at the big chain supermarkets.

A number of the Chinese bachelors married black women and had families, and descendants of those families are still living in the Delta. The children of these families had to attend black schools when public education was segregated. Eventually, Chinese women could come to America more freely and did so. As Chinese families prospered, they raised increasing objections to the education their children were getting, and began sending their children to the segregated white schools. While some people grumbled, the Chinese students were allowed to stay, and many of them immediately went to the top of their classes. When the Supreme Court desegregated the schools, and the white students were withdrawn, the Chinese went with them and sent their children to the academies. Chinese-Americans in the Delta have always put a high premium on education, and for many years some of the area's best scholars have been Chinese-American.

The ancestors of the Delta's substantial Jewish population often arrived as peddlers who settled to a mercantile life downtown, like the Chinese, but the Jewish merchants usually dealt in clothing. All three clothing stores on Main Street in Indianola are owned by Jewish families, the first of which opened in 1912.

Indianola's Jews drive to the synagogue in Greenville for services.

In fact, Greenville's synagogue had the largest membership in Mississippi until 1980, when the Jackson synagogue surpassed it, not because of growing numbers of Jews in the state capital, but because the Delta was losing numbers of all of its racial and ethnic groups. For a young person in the Delta with a good mind who is unlanded, there are very few opportunities. They make their way out into the world, from Maine to California and everywhere in between, and they only go home to the Delta for Christmas or Hanukkah.

There are Jewish farmers in the Delta, as well as shopkeepers. The Jews who settled there, whether to work the land or sell dry goods on Main Street, do not grant much more respect to dark-skinned Deltans than the paler Gentiles around them, although they are slightly more tolerant. Or, maybe, just more practical.

Ed Scott remembered an incident during the Freedom Summer of 1964, when people were being registered to vote and a bunch of white farmers around Drew and Ruleville got together to talk about how they would deal with it. They decided to use herbicides on the cotton in great quantity, so that they would not need black people to keep the weeds out of the fields. The idea was to take away their work as a warning about what would happen if they continued registering.

"That was one way of retaliating against black people, and when everyone went to register to vote, the white farmers got together and said, 'Let's use chemicals and don't give 'em no work to do on the farm,'" Scott said. "There was a Jew around here named Sidney Livingston who had more land than anybody, and when they had a meeting one night to talk about not letting people chop cotton or make money, Sidney asked, 'What if it starts raining and you can't get your chemicals out?' They said, 'Well, we'll just have to take that chance.'

"Sidney said, 'I tell you what y'all do. Take y'all's meeting and go to hell, and I'm gonna take my niggers and put them in the field.' That's just the way he said it, and he took all those hoe-hands and put them in his field the next morning and nobody bothered him."

Jews in the Delta are practically indistinguishable from their Gentile counterparts. The men hunt and fish. Jewish women complain with as much distress and frequency as their Christian neighbors about not being able to find good help to keep their houses clean at minimum wages without benefits. (Domestics work for less in the Delta than just about anywhere in the country, judging by the large numbers of fifty- and sixty-year-old women I saw cleaning houses for $3.65 an hour.)

But for all the assimilation, there is still a certain markedness to being Jewish. "There's not much anti-Semitism," one merchant from Indianola told me. "But just when you're going along thinking that it's all behind you, something happens. Our daughter had an incident at school last year. There'll always be something to remind you."

For more than sixty years there has been a prominent Muslim family in Belzoni—the Mohameds—still there today, still influential in the community. Hassan Mohamed, a Lebanese immigrant, met Ethel Wright in the Delta town of Shaw in 1923 and married her the following year. Her family in Beirut is as close to her as her family here, she said. She had visited them in Lebanon and they had been to Belzoni. She remained a Christian, she told me, but her husband was a Muslim and her sons were also Muslims. "I was never much for church-going."

In 1928, the young family moved to Belzoni and opened H. Mohamed's Dry Goods, which grew and prospered, as did their family. Their son Bubba Mohamed grew up to own a store in Inverness and another son, Ollie, has one in Belzoni. Ethel and Hassan had a family of eight children. Then, in 1965, Hassan died. By then, all the children had grown and left home. Big Mama, as Ethel Wright Mohamed is affectionately known to family and friends, was lonely.

"It was the first time I'd ever been alone," she told me. "The house had always been full. I was depressed. I was keeping the store, so I was all right during the day 'cause I had something to do, but the nights were long."

When I met her, Ethel Wright Mohamed was eighty-three years old. She was a well-known folk artist whose stitchery work hangs in the Smithsonian. She has white hair, lively blue eyes, and a square build, but not so large as to account for why she is called Big Mama. She works in a beautiful sunlit studio behind her house, glass-walled and surrounded by morning glories, which bring a constant traffic of hummingbirds.

"I was so alone. I wanted to write down all of my memories, but I'm not a writer. Then I tried painting, starting out with stick men and filling them in with my brush. I saw it was going to be fun. I was fifty-nine and I felt like I would never be happy in my life again, but this made me smile. Every night when I got home I'd get out my brushes and paints and start drawing whatever occurred to me.

"My grandson told me my painting was weird, so I started embroidering to hide it. I found that was even more calming than painting. I never thought anyone who knew anything about art would like my work. I thought, It's just me."

But, it was not just her. The people and places she embroiders, drawn from her memory and imagination, are alive, reaching out from the cloth. She does not sell her work, but donates two or three pieces a year to be auctioned off for one or another charity. They often fetch more than $7,000 apiece.

The newest ethnic group to fan out and dig in across the Delta are people from India, many of them with roots close to Bombay. They settle into the business of buying motels and managing them. Almost every motel in the Delta is operated by an Indian family. To register for a room in a Delta motel is to be treated to a delightful noseful of the most redolent curry imaginable. Dark-skinned, beautiful children watch gravely as you stand there and fill in the registration card, their eyes dark pools, while a woman in a sari takes your money. There are no East Indians in the country club, but they are welcome to send their children to the Academy, if they can afford it.

My amazement at the Delta sunsets never ceased. As Tony Dunbar observed in *Delta Time*, it is a land so vast, flat, and treeless, that when the sun starts to slip below the horizon, even the dirt clods in the fields cast shadows. With so few trees between the fecund earth and the sun, the dying light suffuses huge tracts of land, the air itself seeming to soak up the pastel colors of the sky, above the deep, shadowed brown of the soil.

One night, coming back from Jackson to Indianola on Highway 49, I headed down out of the bluffs of Yazoo City and crossed the Yazoo River, coming off the bridge on to the flat table of flood plain where the land suddenly levels out and the Delta begins as clearly as if there were a billboard announcing it. The sun was just going down, golds and pinks spilling across the land. The highway crossed a bayou, and from the bridge I saw gaunt cypresses standing in dusky water that was tinged a rippling pink by the sunset. Clouds swirled across the huge sky, their undersides lit by a sheen of color. Three small, white egrets flew in a V-formation across the road. Even the water in the grudge ditch along the highway was a delicate rose pink. It is always a surprise to encounter sunsets of such subtle colors in the middle of those vast acres, where things and feelings generally get writ large, and subtlety is rare.

CHAPTER IX

The Catfish Blues

IF CHANNEL catfish are allowed to live out a goodly portion of their natural lifespan, they grow into big fish. Most Deltans have seen a huge catfish, up in the thirty- or forty-pound range, at some time in their lives. It seems as if every family has photographs of men in a yard, kneeling down behind a catfish stretched out in the dirt that is longer than the three men kneeling side by side behind it, their pale faces diffident in front of the camera, cigarettes hanging from the corners of their mouths, smoke rising into squinting eyes, looking nonchalant behind that immense fish on the ground in front of them.

At the Magnolia Fish Market in Greenville, the catfish arrive from the Mississippi River, and the river is always full of surprises. There

are people who still fish the river to earn or augment their livings, and when they come to sell their catches to the Magnolia they bring in vastly different sizes, species, and muddy, mottled colors. Forget the farm-raised variety, each fish as uniform as a McDonald's burger, truckloads of catfish all the same. Linda Horton, who owned the Magnolia when I met her, bought what they brought in and processed it on the premises. In the market's front room is a meat case with glass in the front, and inside are gar steaks, buffalo fish, and catfish, skinned and gutted, but with the heads still on.

The Magnolia is in other hands now: Linda Horton died not too long ago by her own hand after a bout with cancer, but when I met her she was ready for whatever someone had to sell. She was a big woman, not very tall, but brawny, with a big body, hefty forearms, and strong, square hands. The first time I went into the shop, a buzzer hooked up to the front door went off, and Linda came out of the back room to see who it was, a bloody towel wrapped around her forearm. She had just punctured herself with the point of a knife, she told me, and thought she might have hit an artery the way it was bleeding. Nonetheless, she offered to show me how to clean a big catfish and led me into the back room.

There were three or four other bloody towels tossed in a corner. "Damn, I hope I didn't hit an artery," she muttered. "I've only had to go to the hospital once. I stuck myself on a bad gar bone and got blood poisoning, with those red lines running up my arm and all."

She showed me how to dress catfish. There was a steel hook hanging from the ceiling with a twelve-pound yellow catfish on it, impaled through the gills and mouth. I followed her instructions, first making knife cuts around the gills, then breaking the dorsal and pectoral fins off with a pair of pliers, which I also used to grab a flap of skin and pull it down. Dressing a catfish is really more like undressing it, like peeling a piece of skin-tight clothing off someone. It takes a steady downward tug on the pliers, and I could feel it in my forearms. A day of doing this would build up anyone's muscles. Linda's biggest day so far had been 2,500 pounds, she told me. She had

worked six years at the Magnolia for her ex-father-in-law. When he wanted to get rid of the market, she had bought it.

The bleeding from her arm seemed to be slowing down. There was a walk-in freezer in the back room and a large aluminum table where she worked on the fish. On the dressing table was a thirty-five-pound channel catfish, skinned and gutted, with a pile of liver next to it. "There's at least two pounds of liver there," she said. "I save it for particular customers."

Catfish are always a steady source of protein for Delta families, and can be counted on to put meat on the table. That may have been one of the important reasons for the pre-Columbian settlements along the Mississippi and Yazoo Rivers of people willing to endure the rigors of the river bottom's swamp land, its mosquitos, and panthers—they could camp beside a large natural icebox that always had something in it. Catfish were part of the diet of the mound builders, the Native American tribes who are now extinct, but who left behind giant earthen mounds. There are still a few of these strange monuments in the Delta that have not been bulldozed, and they swell up suddenly out of the land, narrow hills covered with trees on the top. Around 1500 B.C., when the Yazoo River was part of the Ohio River, the mound builders came to the Belzoni area to stay by the river. They developed a civilization and culture that flourished for more than two thousand years before the Europeans' arrival made the mosquitos lethal instead of just an annoyance, feeding them blood loaded with fevers and diseases previously unknown on this continent.

Like the Native Americans, the white and black settlers ate a lot of catfish, and every little town used to have an equivalent of the Magnolia Market, a place where fish were bought and sold. Catfish provide a part of the diet and a part of the income for poor people in the Delta. Blues singer and folk artist James Son Thomas was sixty-

seven when I met him. He had been raised near the Yazoo River and the men in his family used to run trotlines and sell their catch, as did the men in many families. It was just one more way to get by. Catfish, for him, were formidable animals, nothing to encounter lightly.

"I can remember when I was just a child, seeing them come up to the top of the river, all you'd see were their backs and they were as big as that door yonder," he told me, indicating with a nod of his head the six-foot-high door that shut his bedroom out from the living room in front of it in his small, three-room, shotgun home on a back street of Leland, twenty miles west of Indianola. "When you're a boy, you don't mess with catfish that size."

Thomas worked most of his life as a grave digger in Leland, and he supplements his meager retirement income with sales of his art. He makes ceramic sculptures of animals and people, but his best-sellers, appropriately enough for a man who spent his working life in a graveyard, are the ceramic skulls he fashions. His signature in the folk art world is that he uses real teeth in the skulls, and people who know him or his work send him bags of teeth from places all around the globe. His work is carried by upscale galleries in the Northeast and Southwest, and the Smithsonian has included him in its shows.

I went to see him at his house. The bedroom was small, hot, and stuffy. He sat on his unmade bed, talking and playing, not a drop of sweat on his brow, while I sat amazed at his bottleneck blues licks, wiping my face. On a rickety shelf, a small black-and-white TV gave us "The Flintstones" with the sound off, and up in another corner, by no means prominently displayed, was a picture of former first lady Nancy Reagan shaking Son Thomas's hand.

"I don't know what to tell you about catfish," he said. "We ate a lot of them when I was growing up. I do a song called, 'Catfish Blues.'"

He picked his guitar up off the bed and sang: "If the river was whiskey, I was a diving duck / If the river was whiskey, I was a diving duck / I would swim to the bottom, Lord I would not come up."

The fact was, when I met him, Son Thomas had finished with whiskey after a lifetime of some pretty serious drinking. In 1987, he fell asleep on the floor in his girlfriend's living room, and somehow in the night rolled into a space heater, starting a fire with himself as the main combustant. He was badly burned and spent a month in the hospital in Greenville. He stopped drinking when he got out.

Delta residents banded together to help out with a lot of Son Thomas's hospital expenses. He was, after all, just about the last living country bluesman of his generation, a surviving elder from a group whose chances for long life are slim. Sonny Boy Williamson, Muddy Waters, Howlin' Wolf, Otis Spann, and a host of others had all gone on before him. For many years he played with Sam Chatham, who died in the mid-1980s at the age of ninety.

Son Thomas never made much money from the blues although he played most of his life. The only way his music contributed to his income was when he was hired to play at parties, which he was by white and black alike for many years. He could frequently be found at a soiree anywhere from Greenville to Greenwood sitting in a corner and playing the blues, perhaps with his guitar plugged into a small amp, depending on the size of the room. The blues is background music in the Delta, and he frequently played below the level of conversation. Before he was burned, he got to his dates on his own, but afterward he stopped driving and the host of the party had to come pick him up, bring him to the gig, then take him back to Leland when it was over. He did not make much money for an evening's work.

I first saw Son Thomas at the fourth annual Catfish Races, which were held in a big field next to the offices of the *Delta Democrat Times* on the outskirts of Greenville. Proceeds from the Saturday event went to the local burn center. In one corner of the field, under a lone tree, were a half dozen, long, plastic raceways with water in them for the fish to race through from one end to the other. Each catfish had been subscribed to by a local business, and each business's name

was read over the loudspeaker before every round of races. A few rows of bleachers were erected where people could sit and watch the fish swim down the raceways, and there were about fifty folks sitting there, eating, drinking, and listening to the announcer bark out the races.

Out in the middle of the field, on a flat-bed trailer under the bright sunshine, Son Thomas was sitting on a folding chair, playing his guitar and singing. It was almost noon and killer-hot. He had been playing since 10 A.M. without a break, and was scheduled to be up there until 2 P.M. During most of those four hours he would sit there wrapped in a dark sport jacket with a wide-brimmed black hat on his head. He was not sweating. This is a man with the chill of the grave deep in his bones. He has a dark and deeply marked face, a few snaggle teeth. He had his amp and a microphone, but you could not hear him well until you crossed the field away from the catfish races and stood near the truck. He was well into "Good Morning Little Schoolgirl," when I walked up, and there was only one man standing by the flat-bed listening.

Son Thomas slipped his chrome bottleneck on his little finger and slid into his beautiful and haunting composition, "After the Rainbow." When he was done, the two of us in the audience clapped loudly, and we drew a nod of thanks from him before he leaned into the microphone to do another song. The middle-aged man beside me was wearing a cap from a local hardware store, and he was sweating heavily, the dark mahogany of his face gleaming. He had a wide smile with a big laugh.

"My daddy came up with the greatest of the blues singers, a fellow called Howlin' Wolf," he told me. "They both grew up not too far from here. My daddy told me that Howlin' Wolf used to walk the dirt roads down there at night with his guitar around his neck, singing and howling, and that's how he got his name.

"Thirty years ago, Howlin' Wolf came back here when he was already famous. He came down to Greenville and played at a club on Nelson Street, then he went on over to the VFW hall and played

some more. Me and my daddy went over there and when we came in Howlin' Wolf stopped the show. He said, 'Hold on now, here's a son of a bitch I ain't seen in a long time.'

"My daddy was a deacon in the church by then, but he stepped right up and said, 'I ain't seen you for a long time either, mother-fucker.' Then they wrapped their arms around each other in a big hug."

He laughed and laughed, as Son Thomas launched into "Another Mule Kicking in My Stall."

When I visited Son Thomas at his home he told me that his entire monthly retirement income from his years as a grave digger was $97.50 a month, and he was still paying $47 a month to the Greenville Hospital and the burn center. His house note was over $100 a month, so even if he did not need to buy food, his monthly Social Security check was not enough to cover the bills. Fortunately, his music and his art kept a little extra coming in and that made the difference. Still, he was careful about spending money.

"I'll eat catfish if someone brings me a mess of them, but I don't buy them at the store," he said. "They're too high."

Farm-raised catfish cost more money than Son Thomas's budget allows him to spend in order to put meat on his table, but in most parts of the country consumers are used to spending a little more for seafood than for other kinds of meat. Once people try and like catfish, three or four dollars for a pound of filets does not come as a big surprise at the checkout counter. In 1990, catfish was the fifth most consumed seafood in the United States, outselling salmon, crab, and sole.

This remarkable success, which grew from nearly nothing only twenty years before, has been due in large part to the vertical integration of the industry. The absence of such structure was often an important factor in the failure of other aquacultural endeavors. Just

because you can grow and harvest something in the water does not mean you can profitably process or market it. For many people around the world, fish farming has proved to be a deep hole into which a lot of their money disappeared. There are as many ways to lose money fish farming as there are fish farmers. Often what looks good on paper just does not work out well down on the farm, and the animal turns out to be harder to grow, or process, or sell than anticipated.

Take salmon, for instance. It seemed like a logical aquaculture for the citizens of Oregon and Washington. Pacific salmon such as the chum, coho, and chinook are relatively plentiful, and a good market exists for them, built up over time by the people who fished for them in the ocean. There was a salmon-processing industry already in place to handle those catches, and salmon was familiar to consumers.

The first salmon farms in the Northwest appeared around 1968. The idea was to trap salmon as they came up the freshwater rivers from the ocean to spawn, collect their eggs, hatch and raise the fish, then release them to return to the ocean. Hopefully, the next spawning season, they would all come back upstream to spawn again, then they could be harvested, while the newly spawned generation was raised for the same process. By the mid-1970s, multinational corporations like Weyerhauser and British Petroleum were investing in "salmon ranches." In addition, many coastal residents began small ranching operations, often simply serving as hatcheries, collecting the eggs and selling them to the ranches.

At first, there were good spawning runs of salmon with plenty of eggs available. But then came some bad years, with small egg collections and low rates of returning fish. The numbers of hatcheries and ranches declined and, by 1984, the press reported that $50 million had been spent without one ranch making a profit, although some people were able to say they had lost less than others.

A number of problems bedeviled the salmon ranchers in addition to the small runs and a decline in the numbers of fish. There were

frequent outcries from the holders of commercial and recreational fishing licenses, who believed fish farmers were getting better treatment from the state legislators and regulators then they were. Further, because of the short supply of eggs, many were brought in from out of state, and environmentalists warned that the gene pools of those fish that had been coming up particular coastal rivers since time immemorial would be lost forever when privately hatched fish, whose ancestors hailed from other places, began mixing with the wild stock.

By 1990, Atlantic salmon had replaced the traditional Northwest varieties, and the environmentalists' worries were heightened as this wholly new species thrived in the salmon ranches. Its presence was a direct result of the success that Norwegian, and later Scottish, farmers had in raising Atlantic salmon. In 1974, 2 million pounds of salmon were grown in Norway. By 1990, that figure was more than 250 million pounds.

The fish are grown in huge net cages in the ocean along the Norwegian coast. In 1990, there were more than eight hundred Norwegian salmon farmers. Most of them were families with a long tradition of fishing, and they were already accustomed to capturing, transporting, processing, and marketing large quantities of fish. They readily made the transition from hunter/gatherers to farmers. Salmon farming plugged itself into a vertical fish industry that was already in place.

On a well-managed salmon farm, according to the Norwegian Fish Farmers association, the ratio of feed to meat is one-to-one: a pound of salmon meat is produced for every pound of feed used. While feed costs are borne by both catfish farmers and salmon farmers, there are problems unique to each of the aquacultures. In a net cage, with its relatively small size, there is a problem with sediment building up from feces and uneaten feed, but there is no problem with aeration, because the net cages are in the ocean, where there is always a sufficient exchange of water to keep oxygen levels high.

Scottish farmers began growing Atlantic salmon only a few years

after the Norwegians, and, in 1990, produced about 40 million pounds. One reason posited for the relatively small size of the Scottish effort compared to Norway's was that a much larger number of Scottish salmon farming operations are owned by large corporations and simply managed by farmers, as opposed to the Norwegian model, where most of the farmers work for themselves. In 1990, Norway produced four out of every five Atlantic salmon grown. In the same year, the United States imported well over 100 million pounds of Atlantic salmon.

Norwegian salmon farming is one of the most successful cage aquacultures in the world, but is by no means the first. Of course, for centuries, people have been keeping their fishing catches alive in cages until the fish could be gotten to a market. But the first true cage aquaculture in which fish were bred and raised in a cage until ready to be eaten is thought to have taken place toward the end of the nineteenth century in the waters of Cambodia's Lake Kampouchea. Among the three kinds of fish grown by those first caged-fish farmers was the Cambodian catfish. The first cage aquaculture of fish on a business scale was probably the farming of yellowtail tuna by the Japanese in the 1930s. In 1990, there were over three thousand yellowtail farmers in southern and southwestern Japan, producing a total of about 300 million pounds of fish a year.

In the United States, cage aquaculture has been tried with such diverse species of seafood as lobster, salmon, and tilapia. The latter is a hardy fish, which feeds on algae and is farmed extensively in the Third World, primarily in Africa and the Middle East. Its meat is nutritious, with a sweet, mild taste, and it can grow in colder water than catfish.

Oriental peoples seem to have been much more successful at cage aquaculture than Occidentals, who have tended more toward aquaculture in ponds or raceways. Before catfish, the only fish grown as meat in North America that made a serious profit was trout, which is farmed primarily in southern and central Idaho. Trout has a long history as a popular choice for aquaculture in the First World. It

adapts well to cold climates and produces a good meat with a fine flavor in a fairly short period of time. In the United States, the first trout farming was done in raceways and ponds during the early 1930s. In Europe, however, trout have been raised for centuries in a number of countries, including Italy, Germany, and Austria. In the Soviet Union, trout is still called, "the czar's fish," and has been farmed since the 1880s.

Trout has an excellent feed-to-meat conversion ratio, and requires only one and a half pounds of feed to produce a pound of meat, compared to two pounds for catfish. Nevertheless, with all its advantages, trout farming has never approached the revenue levels of catfish. In 1990, about 57 million pounds of trout was produced in the United States, worth about $64 million.

That was the same year Randy MacMillan went from working on catfish to working on trout. He was hired away from his catfish research at Mississippi State University to the bottom of the Snake River canyon in central Idaho, where he became director of research and development for the Clear Springs Trout Company, the world's leading producer of farm-raised trout. Clear Springs produced 18 million pounds of trout in 1990, a third of the United States' total. The trout are grown in raceways, 118 feet long and 20 feet wide.

"Clear Springs is a vertically integrated company," Macmillan said, when I talked to him by phone after his job change. "They make their own feed, have their own brood stock, grow their own fish, market them, and distribute them. The reason they haven't been able to match the successes of catfish farmers is that the industry doesn't have the marketing organization. The trout people haven't been able to penetrate markets like the catfish people have. There are too many markets they haven't been able to push into, too many parts of the country they haven't been able to penetrate."

Catfish farmers are not satisfied to have done better than trout. They see themselves as part of a newborn industry that is not even approaching its potential. They are only at the beginning. Their standard for success is the chicken industry. It is no wonder. Be-

tween 1970 and 1987, the per capita consumption of chicken in the United States rose from 40.1 pounds to 62.7 pounds per year. During the same period, the average American's increase in consumption of seafood went from 11.8 pounds to 15.4. That leaves a lot of room for improvement as far as catfish farmers are concerned.

The catfish industry has advanced in fits and starts. Each time it looks as if catfish sales have reached a saturation point and will never advance beyond being just another specialized regional food, or will simply become another failed aquaculture, circumstances conspire to keep the industry growing. In the early days, it helped to have county agent Tommy Taylor constantly prodding, poking, and pulling the farmers along. During the 1970s, the amount of underwater acres grew very slowly, particularly during the latter half of the decade, when profits for row croppers were up and the acreage farmed in cotton and soybeans was increasing annually. Taylor was a major resource for struggling catfish farmers, and he approached his job as Humphreys County Extension Service agent more as a mission than a bureaucratic sinecure.

If fish were dying in a pond at 2:30 A.M. and no one could figure out why, Humphreys County farmers knew they could call Tommy Taylor and he would get up and come right over. No matter if "right over" was twenty miles away and down five miles of dirt road in the humid dead of a mosquito-filled night. Over the years of slow sales, farmers refined their methods, pushing the numbers of fish they stocked per acre steadily up, from around two thousand in the late 1970s to six or seven thousand by 1990. Taylor was always there, addressing the real problems, listening to his constituency, and working with them. By the early 1980s, farmers were capable of producing catfish in numbers that could meet a rising national market, if the demand arose. Taylor may have been the first county agent in the history of the extension service, which operates in all fifty states, to have participated in the birth and growth of a $90 million farming industry in his county.

In the early 1980s, however, the catfish industry went into a stall.

It appeared that demand for the fish had reached either a plateau or a peak. Annual sales stayed at about 150 million pounds from 1982 through 1984. Plants were paying farmers only a little more than sixty cents a pound for their fish, and sixty cents was considered the point below which a farmer lost money. In some cases, farmers who were already floundering found the revenues from their ponds were simply not enough to cover their debt service. They had too many fish in the ponds that had to be fed and nowhere to sell them. In Sunflower and Humphreys counties, twenty-six catfish farmers got out of aquaculture. It was the first time in twenty years that the number of Delta acres under water declined. There was a catfish farmers organization in place, the Catfish Farmers of America's Mississippi chapter, but it was not much of a marketing agent. World Catfish Day in Belzoni was about the limit of the CFA's promotional imagination.

Ironically, the catfish industry was rescued from these doldrums by its role model: chicken. In 1985, Church's Fried Chicken—a national fast-food chain—concluded from focus groups that its customers were ready for fried catfish. Catfish became available in more than 1,500 Church's franchises around the country, primarily in the South and Southeast, and many of them were draped with banners across the front of their stores reading: DON'T BE CHICKEN, EAT OUR CATFISH. Church's signed contracts with six processors for a total of about 54 million pounds of fish, more than a third of 1984's entire production. The contracts with Church's resuscitated the industry and boosted catfish production to record levels. But, in 1987, there was bad news. Catfish was not selling in the anticipated numbers, and Church's did not renew its contracts with the processors.

"I think the problem was we didn't market it hard enough," said Bob French when I called him up to ask him. He was with Church's then and had stayed with it through a couple of ownership changes. When I reached him, he was a regional director of operations, based in San Antonio.

"It was a little more expensive than our regular menu, and the

pieces could have been a little too small. And we lacked the marketing skills to sell it. A combination of pricing and marketing resulted in the demise of the product."

In 1987, without Church's to make up the slack, farmers were once again faced with having a lot of fish in their ponds and not enough plants that wanted to buy them. This time, Bill Allen was the man on the spot. A brown-haired, boyish-faced Ole Miss graduate in the Class of 1973, he has a genius for marketing, which might have gone untapped had it not been for catfish. When he got back home to Belzoni from Ole Miss, he began farming the family land. Later he got out of farming and became a commodities broker, in the same offices on Belzoni's Main Street where his father had run a fertilizer distributorship. In 1990, those offices were the world headquarters of the Catfish Institute, of which Allen was the executive director. He is an outgoing, easy person to talk to, and there is an air about him that is encountered frequently among the fair-haired graduates of Ole Miss, an Ivy Leagueness, graceful and full of the noblesse oblige of privilege. Allen is equally at home with a bunch of catfish farmers at the Pig Stand, Governor Ray Mabus in Jackson, or writers from *The New Yorker* magazine at a trade show in Manhattan.

"I farmed full-time from 1973 to 1983," he told me when I went to see him in his Belzoni office, leaning forward on his broad desk, which was covered with bright, four-color press kits about Mississippi Prime catfish and copies of national magazines like *Cosmopolitan* with ads in them for farm-raised catfish, touting it as an upscale but affordable delicacy. "When I stopped farming, I formed a commodity brokerage company here in 1983, trading commodity futures with a brokerage company in Saint Louis, and I was doing business with a good number of these catfish farmers and feed mill people, plus I knew them all from just living here."

In 1986, Allen did not like what he saw in the futures business and sold his brokerage firm. At the same time, the Catfish Farmers of America decided something had to be done in the face of Church's

impending pull-out. The CFA reached an agreement with two of the area's feed mills—Delta Western in Indianola and Producer's Feed in Belzoni—that for every ton of catfish feed they sold, six dollars would be set aside for advertising and marketing catfish. Two CFA directors came to Allen and asked him to administer those funds.

"I told them, 'Okay, let's try it.' I didn't ask for a contract, just for two months' notice if they got tired of me, and I said I'd do the same for them. We still have the same contract," he laughed.

Allen and the CFA created a new, independent entity, The Catfish Institute. In 1987, Allen hired a public relations agency in New York, and the Institute initiated a $1.3 million advertising campaign, targeted at magazine readers between the ages of twenty-five and forty-four, who were making over $30,000 a year. Ads were placed in *Time, Newsweek, Readers Digest, Ladies Home Journal* and *People*.

Shortly thereafter, unpaid media attention began to turn to farm-raised catfish. Articles about them began to appear in places like the *New York Daily News*, the *Washington Post*, and the *Los Angeles Times*. Catfish were mentioned on talk shows and featured in numerous food sections of daily newspapers. In fact, according to a tracking survey, there were more than 2,100 print, television, and radio stories about farm-raised catfish in 1987, with a comparable advertising value of more than $1.5 million, for which not a nickel was paid.

Allen believes that farmers need to be able to count on getting a decent price for their fish from the processors, so in 1989, taking advantage of the same agricultural exemptions from anti-trust violations that applied to feed mills and processing plants, he formed the Catfish Bargaining Association. About 85 percent of the catfish farmers in Sunflower and Humphreys counties joined it. Association members put a set price per pound on the fish they sold to the processing plants, virtually eliminating the practice of one farmer undercutting another's prices. The processors squawked, but almost all of them eventually signed agreements with the association. In

1990, the association's price for fish ranged between seventy-five and eighty cents a pound. Catfish farmers finished the 1980s strongly, with growth in acreage and production for each year the Catfish Institute was in existence through 1990.

In the summer of 1991, however, the catfish industry ran into some more tough times. Increased competition among processors depressed the price of fish at the wholesale level and reduced sales for each plant. With demand for fish slacking off at the peak of the feeding season, many farmers found themselves in cash-flow binds and defected from the bargaining association, accepting less than the set price for their fish. The pond-bank price from processor to farmer plunged as low as sixty cents a pound, eight cents a pound lower than the current break-even point, and no one was sure where it would bottom out. Farmers and processors predicted that during 1992 there would be a dramatic shake-out of those farms and plants without the capital to get through some tough times. Nevertheless, no one doubted that the downturn would eventually correct itself, and that plenty of people would continue to make money farming fish.

Bobby Whelan, from Indianola, is a bluesman, painter, and school teacher who watched it all happen. He came of age as the catfish industry was just getting started. Many of the men with whom he worked in the cotton fields when he was a teenager were working on catfish ponds or in the plants by 1990. He watched farmers prosper from catfish, while black field hands, like he used to be, still got nothing.

"I've watched catfish farming around here go from a few ponds to what it is today," he told me. "The farmers are making a lot of money, but the people working in the plants and at the ponds are still making low, low wages. It's black people making the thing work, but they're the only ones not making decent money out of it."

Whelan is slim and energetic and almost thirty years younger than Son Thomas, but there are some similarities in their lives. Both play the blues with intense devotion and little pay. Both are also visual artists—Thomas with his ceramics and Whelan with his painting. His murals are all over Sunflower County: in churches, schools, and juke joints, as well as the large canvas mural in the long room on the second floor of the Sunflower County Library in Indianola, where one of the state's most successful literacy programs is administered. Scores of people have learned to read looking at that mural on the wall. It is a history of black people in Sunflower County and includes portraits of the county's heros and heroines: Nelson Dotson, first president of the Indianola NAACP; Fannie Lou Hamer; and Indianola native son and blues singer, B. B. King.

Whelan cannot make a living from his painting, nor from playing his own brand of electric blues with his band, Ladies Choice. He teaches in Indianola at Carver Middle School. "I try to be a role model for my students, to let them know that while it's true Jim Crow is alive and well here in the Delta, an obstacle is nothing but a challenge. I try to teach them that they can do whatever they want."

Whelan had the traditional musical education and upbringing of a Delta blues player. He was raised without a father, by a mother who brought up three kids on what she could save from ten dollars a week cleaning house and cooking for a white woman, in addition to twenty-five dollars a month in federal assistance. As a teenager in the early 1960s, Whelan chopped cotton for three dollars a day. During those same years, he was sneaking out of the house at night to go down to the flats by the railroad tracks on Church Street and stand outside the juke joints, listening through the thin walls to the blues players inside. This constituted his music lessons, along with the occasional kind word or demonstrated chord from friends or relatives who played.

Bobby Whelan grew into a rare sort of person, one who was able to combine study and the thing he studied. He played and partici-

pated in the blues tradition, and he also studied it as an art form and cultural expression. He was able to make the jump between musician and academic, and was one of six people in the state designated a blues scholar by the Center of Southern Folklore in Oxford, Mississippi.

Whelan and Ladies Choice got the call to open for B. B. King during the tenth annual B. B. King Homecoming Day concert in Indianola. King is famous as a blues player all over the world, but he began his working life as a dirt-poor tractor driver on a plantation outside of Indianola. When he was not working on the farm, he was coming into town to play guitar and sing on the street, most often at the corner of Second and Church. When the town wanted to honor him with a plaque, King requested it go on the wall of the building there, and he put his footprints and hand prints in cement on that corner.

B. B. King Day, held each year on the first Saturday in June, is a big deal in Indianola. It is one of the few times that the whole town gathers to celebrate a part of Indianola's black cultural heritage. It is well publicized up and down the Delta, and people drive from as far as Jackson and Memphis for the show, held in the city park across the road from Indian Bayou, next to a graveyard. Most white Indianolans share with the black community a sense of civic pride in King's accomplishments. People are forever telling you that it is his hometown.

Of course, not everyone was so happy about the idea of Indianolans celebrating an ex-tractor-driver-turned-blues-singer. I stopped by Lott's Lotta Freeze out on Highway 82 for an oyster poor-boy sandwich before the concert, and an old white man at the next table asked with contempt in his voice if I was going to hear B. B. King. He did not wait for my affirmative answer before telling me the story he had in his mind to tell me when he asked the question in the first place: "I remember back in the 1940s, when he used to play down on Second and Church. The police would come by and move him along. They wouldn't arrest him, just stop the car for a mo-

ment. One'd get out, slap him upside the head, tell him to move on, and he'd move on."

I asked King about it later that night, and he denied ever having been abused at the hands of Indianola's police. "I did used to play on that corner a lot, but the police never once bothered me."

Bobby Whelan and Ladies Choice got to do their opening set for 1990's B. B. King Day concert, but Bee-bee—as everyone calls him—did not. Ladies Choice took the stage in the late afternoon and laid down a solid set of blues under a threatening sky in which clouds were massing. The crowd gathered in the cooling evening with lawn chairs and coolers. It was the first time I saw white and black Indianolans coming together for a public event, joining together to relax. It was a good crowd, mostly young, no catfish farmers that I recognized, but a lot of people. The mosquitos weren't too bad and there were plates of barbecued ribs for sale.

It looked for a while as if the rain would hold off. But, by the time King's Cadillac pulled into the park with its police car escort, there was not-too-distant thunder rolling across the sky, gusts of a stiff breeze blowing across the park, and frequent flashes of sheet lightning. King's road crew kept glancing apprehensively toward the sky as they set up on stage, following the conclusion of the Ladies Choice set. Finally, as the air rapidly grew cooler, the roadies brought out big sheets of plastic, which flapped in the wind as they covered the banks of amplifiers, the electronic keyboard, and the set of trap drums.

Meanwhile, King's Cadillac was immediately surrounded by scores of little kids, three and four deep, black and white, waiting for a glimpse of King as he stepped out of the rear of the car to walk to the stage. The children of Indianola loved him and he loved them back. The concert, in fact, was a benefit for improvements to Indianola's parks and playgrounds. When King took the stage, the first rows standing closest to the stage were entirely made up of kids. Then, before he could get a song done, the sky opened up and a deluge came down. The electricity to the stage was cut off for safety's

sake, and the King of the blues, big and round, stood there in the rain, wiping not sweat, but rainwater off his head with the white towel in his broad hand, and talking to the kids without a microphone, answering questions from anyone, kids or otherwise, who wanted to shout one up to him: "Bee-bee, why do you call your guitar Lucille? Bee-bee, how many Cadillacs you own? Bee-bee, you got any kids? Bee-bee, how much money do you make?"

On and on, while the rain poured down. Both audience and performer were hanging around, stalling for time in hopes that the weather would change and give them an hour together, but finally no one could think of another question, the road crew had the show broken down and packed up, and King made his way back to the Cadillac.

His next scheduled stop was Mary Shepherd's Club Ebony, where it was midnight before he came out to a packed house. It was a very integrated crowd waiting for him there, and everyone had paid an eight-dollar cover charge—cheap by New York standards, but plenty steep in Indianola. Most of the whites were casually dressed, most of the blacks elegantly and impeccably tailored, but once Bee-bee took the Club Ebony stage, everyone got up and danced, and no one noticed what color their neighbor's skin was or how they were dressed.

CHAPTER X

Missing the Delta

IT IS notable how many black and white Deltans share names. Even during my brief stay I came across frequent examples, such as Reed, Taylor, and Harris. Black and white Deltans are so close they are knit together at the eyebrows. Their ancestors claimed, cleared, and worked the land in the beginning, turning a vast and inhospitable swamp into astonishingly fertile farmland. It beggars the imagination to look across those huge expanses of flat, treeless, planted fields to a distant horizon and try to picture it as it must have been 150 years ago—river bottom land, cypress swamp, and first-growth hardwoods.

The task of clearing it—of taking down that timber and opening up the land—was Herculean. For a while, the wood was harvested by teams of Slavs during the late 1800s and early part of the 1900s, who were hired in New Orleans and brought up to live in the Delta in rude cabins and camps while they cleared the swamps and woods of the oldest and straightest cypresses. These would be hauled to the nearest railroad and shipped out. Other than that, little of the timber was ever used. When the planters cleared the land, they were trying to get at the soil as fast as possible, and once they had enough wood to build their houses and barns, the rest got burned.

"When they got here, they started with the ridges, that was the first thing they cleared," said a sixty-five-year-old white man who had lived all his life in northwest Sunflower County and who took me on a tour of the back roads to see the first forty acres his father bought after moving from the Hills to the Delta in the 1920s. "Cross-cut saw is what cleared this land. Two-man cross-cut saws. And fire. My daddy hired people to clear the land. This country was full of niggers—they call 'em colored people now, but they were niggers to us—and they came in during the summertime to work when the cotton crop was laid by, in between chopping and harvesting. Back in those days, during the Depression, he paid them fifty cents a day to work from can to can't.

"He had 'em start with the ridges and when they came to a big tree, too big to saw, they'd poison it, and after the limbs dropped off they'd burn it. There wasn't much of a market for it in the Depression. They'd clear the smaller stuff out with mules and burn it. They burned up a lot of fine timber clearing this land."

The morning was hot, the sun bright outside, the air conditioner blasting in the wide, new sedan as we cruised down a gravel road between fenced fields. The wooden fences were overgrown with trumpet vines, the bright-orange, horn-shaped blooms hanging from the dark green of the vine. There were lots of mimosas covered with their cloudbursts of delicate pink blossoms, big pecans, and

pines growing close to the roadside. The only trees left standing are those at the very edges of fields. I glanced back every so often to peer out the rear window at the dust cloud of our passage.

We drove a long way, and, finally, the old man pulled off the road in front of a small, wooden house with a short porch on it. In the front yard, just back from the road, was a foot-high block of marble, and on its top was inscribed his father's name, and the date he bought his first forty acres. I could read the inscription from the passenger's seat, but he told me three times to get out of the car and go look at it. Meanwhile, he seemed to be growing somewhat agitated, one hand groping around beneath the driver's seat.

He's feeling around under there for a gun, I thought, he's got something against smart-ass writers from out of state, and he's going to shoot me in the back of the head while I'm standing there looking down at that block of marble. Nevertheless, I got out, walked over, spent the obligatory admiring moment gazing down at the marker and turned back toward the car. His door was open and I saw him putting a small, heavy, lethal-looking pistol with a polished wooden handle in the front pocket of his pants.

Sweat trickled from under my arm and ran down my side. I forced myself to sit back down in the car before asking him as casually as I could, considering the fact we were so far back in the deep Delta that no one would have found my body for a century, why he was arming himself.

It was on account of his brother-in-law who lives in the wooden house, he explained. There was bad blood between them, but if he wanted to see this marker, my God, he was gonna come and see it. There had been threats, he said, but he was ready. He patted his pocket. "My brother-in-law's biggest problem is he's crazy. Always has been."

Family. It oils the engine of life everywhere, but even more so in the Delta. The structure of family may differ slightly from race to race—black Deltans' families are often less nuclear, a father may be absent, but on the other hand uncles, aunts, grandparents, and cousins are more likely to live together under one roof to economize on the cost of shelter—but both black and white are wrapped up in the lives of their blood kin.

Deltans are thrown in on themselves by the land, isolated by nature from the rest of the world, and their families assume tremendous importance. The natural isolation produces a society of people both independent and self-contained. Deltans are rarely truly happy anywhere else, never wholly satisfied by success in other parts of the country, because some part of them belongs in the Delta and never ceases missing it.

They miss the bright sun and turned ground. There is a rhythm and a feel to it that does not exist elsewhere. Small, delightful things are still taken for granted in the little Delta towns, things that are no longer found in most of the rest of America. In restaurants and stores, for instance, blank checks from both of Indianola's banks are still kept by the cash registers. Blank checks! It is no wonder that each year in New York's Central Park, a group of Deltans in exile come together for a party, a simultaneous mourning and celebration at being in New York instead of the Delta.

People who drive at night, for any reason, across the Delta spend a lot of time cleaning their windshields. After sunset, even a short journey can leave a thin film of crushed insect bodies on the windshield. One day I pulled my van into Gresham's service station in downtown Indianola to fill up with gas. In front of me, blocking the pumps, was a big grey Cadillac. Its driver was a young blond woman, her young son standing up on the back seat. She waited in the car, engine idling, air conditioning running, windows up, while the young attendant cleaned her windshield, then she drove off without buying anything, or even rolling down her window to thank

him. He told me she was a steady customer, so he always obliged her when she came in with a dirty windshield.

There is a particular pace to life in the Delta, and those who were raised in it and subsequently left speak of it with longing in their voices. Nevertheless, young Deltans, both black and white, know they have to leave if they want to make something of themselves. They do it regretfully, but they go. Year after year, the small towns lose population and dry up. The best place to look for work is all too often the road heading north out of town. This exodus is the region's worst problem and is fed by all its others—the high rates of poverty, unemployment, crime, and the exceptionally uneven distribution of the area's wealth.

I met a widow from Sunflower, a small town south of Drew in northern Sunflower County, a self-reliant woman with a large, capable mind. She loved her hometown, knew its people and land in detail, but she doubted she would be able to live out her life in Sunflower. Crime is bad in that tiny town, unemployment high, and drug abuse common. The one remaining drugstore in town had just closed, and the main street facing the Sunflower River is just a row of dusty vacant buildings. The only people who are not thinking of leaving are the people too poor to do so, or those making a living from those poor people. There is crack cocaine for sale in this tiny town of under eight hundred residents, and a middle-aged woman living alone cannot help but be anxious. There is an air of post-colonialism in many of these little Delta towns, where European-Americans have been forced to either adapt to the loss of absolute power or leave. When whites relinquish the power they have held so long, they insulate themselves with their wealth or relocate—either way effectively abandoning the town.

If the Delta is not to dry up and disappear like the boarded-up stores in Sunflower, its citizens must all take some responsibility for transforming it from Third to First World. White and black must cooperate, work together, and reclaim it as Deltans, ignoring the color of their skin. If the Delta is to do more than survive, if it is to

nourish its children rather than lose them, the people living there must reclaim their right to prosper on that land by working together—this time not as master and slave or tenant and land-owner, but as equals. The Delta is in need of salvation, redemption, reclamation.

The lowly catfish could be that instrument of salvation. The successful introduction of a new staple into the American diet, particularly a new kind of meat, is very rare. American livestock has consisted of basically the same species for a long time. Catfish are poised to make the leap between being an agricultural oddity with a specialized market to something turning up regularly in grocery baskets and fast-food franchises across the country. If catfish can make that transition, its potential worth could provide the Delta with the means to elevate life for all of its citizens.

Catfish have a long history of being eaten by the Delta's residents. Archaeologists have determined that the Delta was occupied, particularly on its river banks, from the Poverty Point culture of 2000 B.C. through the Mississippian tribes of 1200 A.D. Catfish bones are found in plentiful quantities in the middens, the garbage dumps, of most of these cultures. And the catfish has been used for more than its meat. The sharp spines were used as sewing needles by members of the Densonville culture, which flourished from 300 to 800 A.D. Archaeologists have turned up spines with a hole bored in one end for the thread.

Is it too much of a reach to declare that the catfish could sew the Delta back together? Fish farming is generating new revenue, and some of it could be used to lift up the Delta and all its people. The plants could open the ranks of their management jobs to black people and provide workers with favorable working conditions that would allow them to prosper and have a stake in their own lives. It is at the labor-intensive level of processing that the greatest opportunities exist to help the underclass and at the same time do something to ease up on the conditions that force some into lives of crime and drugs. The plants could give employees stock options and day

care, and use some of the profits to help the local community beyond the level of offering minimum wage and benefits and sponsoring Dixie Youth Association baseball teams.

White Delta farmers are not exactly received with open arms at local banks when they came to ask for a loan so they can dig and stock a few ponds, but their reception is cordial when compared with that of the black farmers in Sunflower and Humphreys counties. They are simply not able to get loans. And, while the federal government is prepared to help cotton farmers with giveaway subsidy programs, there are no federal programs that will loan money to the black Delta farmer who wants to put some ponds on his land. The livelihoods of many white farmers are in jeopardy, but their problems pale next to those of the handful of surviving black American farmers. Those few left deserve some help.

In 1990, none of this showed much promise of happening, and Deltans continued to immigrate to other parts of the United States. Yet there is something about the land and the life in the Delta that continues to call to them, tugging at some deeply buried part of them. Only the Delta's siren song can explain why even black people with college educations and plenty of prospects elsewhere sometimes return.

"I came back for my children," said Malcolm Walls. "I was born and raised in Clarksdale and went to Tougaloo College in Jackson, and then, like many southerners, I decided to leave and go North. I went to Detroit and ended up working in New York and living in Westchester County. But when I started raising a family I decided to come back. It was too impersonal. I had some good economic opportunities there, but I decided to come back.

"There is a distinct difference with people here, in their attitudes. There is something about the culture here and it crosses lines between blacks and whites. The foods, the lifestyle, a lot of the traditions, and in their basic caring and attitude about this place."

A white woman from Sunflower County once told me that white southerners don't mind how close they live to blacks as long as

whites make more money, while white northerners don't care how much money blacks make as long as they don't have to live near them. Malcolm Walls echoed her observations.

"Even though there's as distinct a line of racial division as you could ever imagine here, there's still something about it that's a little bit warmer. And one thing about the racial differences is that people here tend to be upfront about it, and you know who you're dealing with, whereas in Westchester you really didn't know. You had the economic wherewithal to be involved in different things, but you still didn't know where people stood."

Walls is a lean man with a trim moustache who now works in Greenville with Mississippi Action for Community Education (MACE), the organizer of the Delta Blues Festival. MACE has been putting on the festival since 1977, and it now draws some fifteen thousand people to Greenville each year for a day of the blues. It is a good fund-raiser for the nonprofit community action group, and it brings blacks and whites together to pay tribute to the blues, a jewel in the Delta crown.

"There's nothing all that special about the festival," said Walls. "It's an event where people go and relax and entertain themselves and have a good time. But the blues are every day. People here are actually living the blues. It's more than just the musicians, it's a life-style, and for the festival weekend people are able to come interact with the living culture of the blues.

"The original mission of the festival was to get blacks in this area to appreciate their own indigenous art form, which has influenced just about every kind of American music. And that came out of a time of some of the people's worst exploitation and degradation. The people learned to survive, adapt, and transform these messages of survival into the blues. Now it's a powerful commercial entity, but it came out of their power to survive. Think of all the other things that could be done."

Another gem in the crown of the Delta is MACE itself, which was started more than twenty years ago and has served the region's poor

in a variety of ways. The organization owns an office building in downtown Greenville and has bought the old Greenville Hotel across the street and converted it into apartments for senior citizens. Both buildings are on a lonely stretch of Washington Avenue that is otherwise occupied only by an Army surplus store and some boarded-up juke joints. Washington Avenue could be a wonderful thoroughfare—it runs from Highway 82 through the heart of downtown to the Greenville levee and the Mississippi River, the end of the Delta. It has wide sidewalks with planters, streetlights, and plenty of room for pedestrian traffic, but it needs a downtown revitalization that has not happened yet. There are not many people on the streets or in the few stores still open for business, and the folks you do see do not look like they have much disposable income.

"One of the things that has happened since I've been back here is that both blacks and whites are beginning to realize what racism is costing us," Walls told me. "Not only is it costing us in future development, but it costs us in real dollars. The public school system in Greenville is terrible—it's 90 percent black and totally underfunded, while the white kids go to private academies. This costs both blacks and whites.

"Even though blacks and whites do have different lifestyles, there are so many similarities that we have to keep struggling against the stereotypes that have been handed down for so many generations. That's one of the things that MACE has been able to do: demonstrate that blacks are capable of being developers, managers, business people, educators. The hotel across the street is one example of how we view physical development. The idea of these kinds of physical structures is to show people that blacks are capable.

"The catfish industry does offer some solutions, but we have to work hard to change the mind-set of the owners and the industry to pay better wages, to allow some upward mobility in the industry for blacks. Mississippi ranks in the middle of the fifty states for the largest number of millionaires, but its poor are the poorest of the poor. These folks in the catfish industry could pay higher wages. They

could find blacks to put into the upper levels of the management systems, but it's just a very closed system, a closed mentality.

"By not doing this, they perpetuate the present situation in which most of the young minds that are ready to become productive leave the area. We're exporting more teachers than we are cotton. Many of our undereducated young people also go North to the northern ghettoes. We're like a baseball farm team, and we're sending those kids up to the major league ghettos. This causes us to think that if we don't address many of the rural problems here, there'll never be a solution to many of the urban problems, to the ghettoization of the urban underclass."

I didn't realize how accustomed I had grown to living in the Delta until the time came to leave. As I retraced the miles heading east out of Memphis, back across Tennessee and away from the pull of the Mississippi River, the woods and rolling fields that appeared beside the interstate gave me a distinct sense of claustrophobia, as if the landscape and all the possibilities it might contain had somehow shrunk. I felt suddenly hemmed in, with my vision blocked.

People who were raised in the Delta and live elsewhere can be bitter about their roots; they may only go back for weddings or funerals and leave even those as soon as it is civilized to do so. In their minds, the Delta is a world behind a wall, where values remain unchanged, ones they cannot share or prosper under. But some part of them never ceases missing a vista with only earth and sky for its boundaries. I feel among their number.

Bibliography

Applebome, Peter. "Caring for the Poorest: A Rural Doctor's Fight." *The New York Times*, Feb. 12, 1990, p. 1.

Autry, James A. *Life After Mississippi*. Oxford, MS: Yoknapatawpha Press, 1989.

Bardach, John E., et al. *Aquaculture: The Farming and Husbandry of Freshwater and Marine Organisms*. New York: John Wiley & Sons, Inc., 1972.

Beveridge, Malcolm C. M. *Cage Aquaculture*. Surrey, England: Fishing News Books, Ltd., 1987.

Blakeslee, Sandra. "Catfish Slime's Healing Agents." *New York Times*, Jan. 26, 1988, p. III:1.

Botkin, Benjamin. *A Treasury of Mississippi River Folklore*. New York: Crown Publishers, 1955.

Brown, David Wayne, ed. *The Delta Initiatives* Memphis, TN: The Lower Mississippi Delta Development Commission, 1990.

Bureau of Information Resources. *Vital Statistics: Mississippi, 1989*. Jackson, MS: Mississippi Department of Health, 1990.

Cahill, Tim. *Jaguars Ripped My Flesh*. New York: Bantam Books, 1987.

Central Delta Academy Parent-Teacher Organization. *The Share-Cropper*. Inverness, MS: Central Delta Academy P.T.O., 1987.

Chesteen, Richard Dallas. "Change and Reaction in a Mississippi Delta Community." Unpublished ms., 1972.

Cohen, Lucy. "Early Arrivals." *Southern Exposure*, July/August 1984, pp. 24–30.

Cohn, David. *Where I Was Born and Raised*. Boston, MA: Houghton Mifflin Co., 1948.

Crawford, Linda. *The Catfish Book*. Jackson, MS: University Press of Mississippi, 1991.

Dollard, John. *Caste and Class in a Southern Town.* Garden City, NJ: Doubleday & Co., 1937.

Dunbar, Tony. *Delta Time: A Journey Through Mississippi.* New York: Pantheon Books, 1990.

Eakin, Frank. "Beyond the Catfish Price Wars." *Seafood Business,* Federal Writers Project. *Mississippi: A Guide to the Magnolia State.* New York: Hastings House, 1959.

Gallagher, Peter B. "A Painful memory of a fish's revenge." *The Atlanta Journal/Constitution,* July 15, 1990, F-6.

Gatewood, Willard B., Jr. *Theodore Roosevelt and the Art of Controversy: Episodes of the White House Years.* Baton Rouge, LA: Louisiana State University Press, 1970.

Halstead, Bruce. *Poisonous and Venomous Marine Animals of the World.* Washington D.C.: United States Government Printing Office, 1965.

Hemphill, Marie. *Fevers, Floods and Faith: A History of Sunflower County, Mississippi, 1844–1976.* Indianola, 1980.

Hermann, Janet Sharp. *The Pursuit of a Dream.* New York: Oxford University Press, 1981.

Hickling, C. F. *The Farming of Fish.* New York: Pergamon Press, 1968.

Hillkirk, John and Gary Jacobson. *Grit, Guts & Genius.* Boston, MA: Houghton Mifflin Co., 1990.

Imes, Bernie. *Juke Joints.* Jackson, MS: University Press of Mississippi, 1990.

Keenun, Mark E. and John E. Waldrop. *Cash Flow Analysis of Farm-Raised Catfish Production in Mississippi.* Mississippi State: Mississippi Agricultural and Forestry Experiment Station, 1988.

Lago, Barbara. "Sonar Project Could Help Keep Tabs on Fish." *The Catfish Journal,* p. 9, October, 1990.

McCall, Michael. "Catfish Makes It To 'Top 5.'" *The Catfish Journal,* August, 1990, p. 8.

McGee, William Mitchell, et al. *Demographic and Attitudinal Characteristics of Catfish Consumers.* Mississippi State: Mississippi Agricultural and Forestry Experiment Station, 1989.

Norwegian Fish Farmers Association. *The Norwegian Fish Farming Industry in Harmony with the Environment.* Trondheim, Norway: Norwegian Fish Farmers Assn., 1990.

Powdermaker, Hortense. *After Freedom: A Cultural Study in the Deep South.* New York: The Viking Press, 1939.

Stranger and Friend: The Way of an Anthropologist. New York: W. W. Norton & Co., 1966.

Riche, Pierre. *Daily Life in the World of Charlemagne.* Philadelphia, PA: University of Pennsylvania Press, 1978.

Sawyer, Charles. *The Arrival of B. B. King.* New York: Doubleday, 1980.

Schweid, Richard. "Delta Strike: Civil Rights or Just Plain Economics?" *Los Angeles Times*, Nov. 18, 1990, p. M:4.

Shapiro, Laura. "Down on the Fish Farm." *Newsweek*, March 25, 1991, pp. 56–58.

Smith, Frank. *The Yazoo River.* New York: Rinehart Publishing Co., 1954.

Smothers, Ronald. "It's Fish Farmers vs. Birds, and Birds Are Winning." *New York Times*, Nov. 5, 1989, p. 26.

Smurthwaite, Don and Neil Armantrout. "Salmon Ranching: The Dream that Got Away." *Northwest Magazine*, June 24, 1984, p. 4.

Starr, Kathy. *The Soul of Southern Cooking.* Jackson, MS: University Press of Mississippi, 1989.

Sugarman, Tracy. *Stranger at the Gates: A Summer in Mississippi.* New York: Hill and Wang, 1966.

Tajima, Renee. "Intersection in the Delta." *Southern Exposure*, July/August, 1984, pp. 18–21.

Taulbert, Clifton Lemoure. *Once Upon a Time When We Were Colored.* Tulsa, OK: Council Oak Books, 1989.

Williams, Greer. *The Plague Killers.* New York: Charles Scribner's Sons, 1969.

Williams, Nathania M. and Abby Sharpe, eds. *The Delta 1990.* Jackson, MS: Department of Mass Communications, Jackson State University, 1990.

Young, Stephen Flinn. "Be In Touch and Stay Cool: The Ladies Choice Band." *Living Blues*, March/April 1989, pp. 22–28.